Volume

Lost in La Dolce Vita

To Jeff & Maria with all my love

Navyo

Navyo Ericsen

Published by Navyo Ericsen
San Anselmo, California, USA

First edition, June 2020

Cover, interior design and photography: Navyo Ericsen
Cover photos: Bronze statue of Danaë, mother of Perseus, by
Benvenuto Cellini, part of the marble pedestal of Cellini's Perseus
Slaying Medusa in the Loggia dei Lanzi, Florence; backstreet in
Perugia, Umbria.
Back cover photos: Inside the Colosseum, Rome; the author in
Palermo, Sicily, June 2013.
Inside photos: San Gimignano, Tuscany; the Colosseum and the Arch
of Constantine, Rome; Mt Vesuvius across the Bay of Naples from
Castello Sant'Elmo, Naples; Palermo, Sicily.

ISBN: 9798647287335

Contact the author at:
NavyoEricsen.com
Facebook.com/NavyoEricsenWriter
Twitter: @navyo

Also available as an ebook.

Neither Couchsurfing.com nor TrustedHousesitters.com have been
involved in the writing or production of this book.

Contents

TUSCANY

Preface

Looking Deeper

My first taste of Italy, as recounted in *Soul Traveler: Taking the Jump*, enraptured me as it would, or should, anyone. I was in childlike wonder at the sensual world around me full of passion, color and history, my feet sometimes barely touching the ground.

Now, after much more experience of the country, I've slowed down, taken more in. That awe and wonder have never left—an impossibility—yet as I've become more accustomed to being in Italy, I'm more open to the details, the minutiae of Italian life that can be both supremely elevating and infernally confounding.

At the beginning of the year this journey took place, while in my native England, I had to deal with feeling lost and adrift in the world. I'd have preferred not to. I even tried to avoid it, but that is not the purpose of my being human or of my travels.

I had no choice. There was something in store for me that I did not expect nor plan for, something far more confronting—my mother's death, a life-changing experience that shaped my future, my travels and how I came to write this book.

After the initial shock, the grieving process became at times debilitating. Two months later when I arrived in Italy, it had become my traveling companion, reminding me of its presence on many an occasion, like it or not.

I had to feel, to look deeper, to become more aware, to use the subtle senses. Each time I felt lost, or literally became lost, was another opportunity. My adventure was not just an outer one, but an inner one.

While this book was in its final stages, the world came to a standstill with the coronavirus pandemic. Travel, especially international travel, was out of the question.

Italy itself became the hardest-hit country in Europe, its hospitals stretched well past their limits. With such a large number of elderly in the population and a family tradition of three generations living together, it's no wonder their casualties were so high.

In light of all this, the story that follows could be seen as a historical document: when close proximity and physical contact were part of life, when budget air travel and packed trains were expected, when standing-room-only bus rides were normal and squeezing into a tiny cafe was fun.

But the ground has moved for all of us. The feelings of being lost and adrift are just as relevant now as they were for me when this journey took place.

Structures we relied upon—our social habits and rituals, the familiarity of regular life—have shifted and for many, disappeared. Identified with those structures, fear, insecurity and loss become magnified.

But it's not ourselves that are changing, it is only the structures around us. Returning to the deeper self, the true core within, the self that never dies—the soul-self—enables us to come back to center, to the ground inside us that is present wherever we are.

Inhabiting that deeper self one finds some surprising truths: we are all connected by a subtle web of relationship; and not just to each other but to the world we live in, to a greater power, to the eternal and infinite.

That journey into self is one I present here in the context of an adventure through Italy—a soul traveler, lost in the sweet life.

Navyo Maxwell Ericsen
Somewhere in Europe

Much of the travel that follows was enabled by the Couchsurfing global hospitality network, where I would stay in the home of my host in an arrangement based on mutual trust, honesty, friendship and cultural exchange.

The Journey

UNITED KINGDOM

Oxford
Ipswich
London

DENMARK

Aarhus
Copenhagen
Aerö

ITALY

Milan

Lucca Fiesole
Pisa Florence
Empoli
San Gimignano Colle val d'Elsa

Rome

Naples
Amalfi
Sorrento Positano

SARDINIA

Palermo

SICILY

N
W E
S

Map not to scale

For my mother, Anna.

Introduction

The
Gift

It was in the cold and snow of England that I started to feel lost. Something had shifted inside me and I had no idea what it was. That confident, assured traveler from last year Couchsurfing his way through Italy was nowhere to be found. Instead, here I was in and around Oxford pulling my heavy bag through the snow like a polar explorer, like my ancestor Hans avoiding frostbite.

It wasn't that I was short of company—all my Couchsurfing hosts were women and I felt cared for during this strange time in an almost maternal way.

One day out and about, a Scandinavian family walked past me, two tall young women, their tall mother and clean-cut well-built father, the sound of their language a reminder of my family heritage and a dream of Denmark.

But I still felt lost. I needed something, something to hold onto.

Soon afterward, that something arrived in my email—a two-month housesit in a small village in Suffolk, not far from my hometown. I applied and confirmed the assignment the next day.

It was here that all became clear.

After settling in the old converted schoolhouse, even with the company of cats and a sweet springer spaniel, I had difficulty focusing on my work, on anything. I felt unmotivated and listless. Within a few days, I got the news.

My brother Richard called and told me our mother, Anna, was in hospital with pneumonia and at her age, she wasn't coming out.

The following day, I received an offer to housesit in Copenhagen. The dream of Denmark suddenly became real and the timing was uncanny. I took it as a sign. Not only that, but here I was in East Anglia, the land of Viking conquests.

My mother's grandfather was from Denmark and she kept strong ties with the Danish side of the family. I decided that when the time came, I would take some of her ashes to Denmark for a memorial. I accepted the housesit and started planning my trip.

But I kept disappearing into a void of inner emptiness and had to let go. I tried filling this void with television, movies, reading, eating, anything that would provide an escape.

At least the BBC provided a glimpse of my future. Italy Unpacked, a food and culture-packed road trip through Italy with its two jovial presenters, art historian Andrew Graham-Dixon and chef Giorgio Locatelli, stirred my passion and my memory and gave me impetus to return.

During a visit to Via Francigena, the old pilgrim's path, they met with a father from the Novalesa Monastery. His words spoke to me.

"A pilgrimage represents the journey of your life where you leave everything behind and set out on your own. You find yourself in places you don't know and face difficulties in order to get closer to God."

Although I'm not a religious man by any means, something deep within me was changing.

I took long walks in the snow, the cold white landscape at times with no distinction between earth and sky a perfect mirror of my inner state.

The feelings of being lost in Oxford now had meaning —something in me had already begun to prepare.

My brothers, Richard and Joff, and I made arrangements to visit Mum in hospital. It was the first time we'd been together since Dad died five years ago.

Seeing her lying in the hospital bed was a shock—her shrunken body, her face gaunt, mouth open, eyes closed. She was clearly dying.

We pulled up chairs and sat around her, touching her, letting her know we were here. Hearing is the last thing to go, they say.

"It's us, Mum. We're all here. Your boys. We love you so much..."

Each of us in turn talked in her ear, telling her how much we loved her, acknowledging her, honoring her, knowing this was the last time we would see her alive.

It was a tearful moment and a powerful bond between brothers being with this fading flesh that bore all three of us.

Two days later, Richard called to say that Mum died in the early morning hours before dawn.

I felt so unknown, so undefined. There were so many mixed emotions brewing beneath the surface, but I didn't know what they were. Everything seemed vague. I just wanted to find a way out of confronting the reality that my mother was dead.

I threw myself into planning my trip to Copenhagen and contacting relatives there, letting them know what happened and finding a place for the memorial. But however much I tried to avoid them, the deep currents of my mother's death stirred within me.

I was faced with the raw, undefinable pain of loss and I couldn't look away.

Crushing headaches disabled me from thinking clearly, from anything, and I had to spend hours sleeping them off. I wanted someone to come and take care of me. I wanted a woman to hold me. I wanted mothering. My body wanted, needed a woman, but she wasn't there. I felt abandoned by my mother, by the feminine, by nourishment, by love.

Nothing mattered. I was alone in the darkness yet I knew that this was where I had to be.

The mourning process has taken me into depths I never imagined. I sense something waiting for me, deep in the abyss. Something life changing, the gift in my mother's death.

Taking her ashes to Denmark was filled with meaning, friendship and a powerful connection to my roots.

I visited the island of Aero where my great-grandfather Alfred and my polar-explorer ancestor Hans were born and raised. I felt the power of the Viking in me. I was introduced to the egalitarian Danish way of life, to the comforts of *hygge*. And I had more bouts of the physical symptoms of grieving. All the while the feminine kept appearing, a continuing thread throughout my travels, showing me I had not been forgotten.

But it was meeting the living, breathing flesh and blood of my mother's forbears that had the most impact. This wasn't history, this was real. I wasn't a visitor anymore, I was one of them.

The memorial with the Danish side of my family, some I hadn't seen since childhood, some I'd never met at all, was not just a reunion but a completion, returning my mother to the land she so loved—I was bringing her home.

Now, after such an intense period of loss and mourning, I needed a return to life, a resurrection, and I knew there was only one place I could find it.

TUSCANY

An Hour in Florence

Stepping off the train, I pull my bags towards the main concourse of Santa Maria Novella station and notice I'm breathing deeper. I'm arriving not just in Florence, but more inside.

Through the busy concourse, past the crowd staring at the information board, I turn onto platform sixteen for the *deposito bagagli*. Even after being away for so long, I remember where it is.

Freed of baggage, I stride out of the station into a perfect spring day in Florence. There's that expanded feeling again, not just of being somewhere new, but of somewhere deeply familiar: the doors, the streets, the people, the smells and sounds, the light—*I know this place*. It's a profound sense of returning.

The past few months fade into a blur of memory as I feel the connection to my surroundings.

Dodging luggage on the small packed sidewalk, squeezing past stalls of hats, bags and sunglasses, I cut down the side of the church of Santa Maria Novella, past its green-and-white striped stone arches into the wide-open space of Piazza Santa Maria Novella.

Having a church, a piazza and a station all named the same, all next to each other, seems confusing yet normal in Italy.

Two short marble obelisks stand at opposite ends of the piazza, each topped with a black iron *fleur-de-lis*, the symbol of Florence.

Tourists mill about, gaping, pointing, chatting, some with rolling cases in tow, most in sunglasses, all under the spell of Italy.

This is the first place I go from the station. Relax, have some tea or *caffè*. Or gelato. Except today there's no time for that. I'm on a schedule to meet Silvia, my friend and host from last year in Empoli, not too far from Florence, which gives me about an hour to walk around. That hour doesn't do justice to the home of the Renaissance, but I'm not about to turn back.

The Arno is a short walk away and I navigate around more tourists on small sidewalks as historic as the architecture, loose flagstones sticking up like invitations.

Crossing the busy Lungarno that runs alongside the river, I gaze out over the water from Ponte alla Carraia, one of the many bridges that span this romantic artery.

Across the bridge in Oltrarno, narrow streets are filled

with the small workshops of artisans—musical instrument makers, furniture restorers, picture framers, watch repairers. This community of creativity is in marked contrast to the more prominent, more popular, more crowded Florence north of the river. It feels older here, more like the Florence of medieval times.

Another public space opens up before me, Piazza Santo Spirito, the tall facade of its yellow church a backdrop for the theater of the piazza. I sit awhile in its leafy shade. Bars and *ristoranti* line its perimeter; students chill out beside me and over by the fountain giving it a hip, youthful vibe.

Further south, the massive medieval gate of Porta Romana still stands in a section of what was once the old city wall. All roads lead to Rome and this was one of them.

Through its giant arches, traffic snarls in a busy five-way intersection.

A road leading away from this loud polluted mess is guarded on either side—on the left, a lion, the protector of Florence, rests on a globe; on the right, a she-wolf suckles two infants, Romulus and Remus, the founders of Rome.

Passing through this mythical gateway, I enter more leafy shade in a park, the sound of traffic slowly fading into the distance. People walk their dogs, sit under the trees reading today's *giornale*, or wander like me in the tranquil beauty.

A large villa up ahead piques my curiosity, but I'm turned away by a woman sitting inside the loggia. It's the

Art School and I'm clearly neither a student nor a visiting *professore*.

Leaving the peace of the park, back towards the river on Via Romana, the statue of a naked young warrior, missing his spear, stands imprisoned behind columns at the corner of a walled garden; tourists bake in the sun on the sprawling, sloping piazza in front of Palazzo Pitti; drinking water pours from the mouth of a stone face into a curvaceous marble bowl at the end of a busy side street.

Crossing Ponte Santa Trinità, figures representing the seasons preside either end of the bridge; further up, a tall column is topped with Justice, sword in hand, weighing her scales of truth.

Mythical imagery is everywhere. It's as if the entire city is telling a story. The Springtime of the Renaissance exhibition is on at Palazzo Strozzi, maybe that will fill me in.

But that's going to have to wait. I have a train to catch.

Coming Home

The thirty-minute train ride passes quickly as we follow the Arno west to Empoli. Hauling my bags onto the platform, I see Silvia waving from the entrance with that unforgettable smile and make my way to greet her.

Even though it's been nine months since I saw her, time disappears in the moment of friendship. I throw my bags in the car and we drive the few blocks to her house.

Everything has that familiar quality again. Her apartment is spacious yet warm and lived-in. Sitting at her old wooden dining table, we talk about some of the life that happened since last year. I share the process I've been going through with my mother's death and I can feel her listening.

She prepares slices of fresh cantaloupe wrapped in tender prosciutto, a delicious traditional combination, and we talk some more until I hear voices echo in the stairwell.

Her two girls return from school and I present them with chocolate, smiles spreading wide with a 'Thank you!' in unison. They don't stay long, but it's sweet to see them again. Young, full of energy and *la vita*.

While Silvia makes dinner, I tune up her old battered guitar and start to play, giving it my fieriest flamenco and busting strings in the process. With a wave of her hand she tells me not to worry, but I can't and promise to get some new ones tomorrow.

After more connection over hearty *pasta ragù*, Silvia drives me to her family villa in the countryside where I'll be staying the next few nights.

Driving up the dirt road in the dark, we pull into the courtyard. Hauling out my bags, I bid her *buona notte* and unlock the front door in the beam of her headlights before she turns around and the sound of her car fades into silence.

Alone in the quiet of this rustic country house, I take a moment to let it all in.

Is this really happening?

Up familiar stone steps to the bedroom, memories come flooding back from last year.

I sit on the big brass-frame bed, the silence and soft lamplight soothing my weary bones before I crawl under the weight of blankets and close my eyes.

Early morning light casts its gentle gaze through the shutters as if waking me from another life. In a way, it has.

Being here in Tuscany is bringing me deeper into myself, into connection with the world around me. It's that powerful sense of returning I've felt ever since I arrived.

After a shower and shave, I'm ready for a day in Florence.

Barreling up the drive in her Fiat, Silvia picks me up as arranged at a quarter to nine to drop me in Empoli. She has a busy week, yet she's letting me stay here and being my personal taxi driver as well as making me dinner. I detect a strong maternal streak.

Silvia is an interesting and complex woman. With her Persol shades, her black leather jacket and her classic looks, she's not only beautiful, she's a mix of emotions with a powerful undercurrent. Being Italian as well as an actress, that sounds not just normal but necessary.

She tells me there have been stupid men in the past who misused her. Although that could be said about most, if not all women, this must be Italy personified—beautiful mothering women and abusive juvenile men. That may seem harsh, but with centuries of a religion worshiping a nurturing mother and a punishing father, it's not short of role models.

She also tells me how much work it is being a teacher, raising two girls and putting on plays. The woman is a dynamo.

She's already late for school, but insists on dropping me off in town. Spying a couple of students on the sidewalk, she slows down, lowering the window.

"*Arrivo subito,*" she tells them in a low, mock-stern voice.

I so wish I had her as a teacher when I was at school.

Silvia lets me out at the central Piazza della Vittoria and we agree to meet at her house for dinner.

The monumental profile of Nike, Greek goddess of victory, spreads her wings in the middle of the piazza, commemorating the fallen of the Great War. Is her mythic meaning truly appreciated? Or has she just become a pair of shoes?

I enter one of the many cafes bustling with morning life, chinks of ceramic cups on saucers interjecting the noisy chorus, and order *un caffè e cornetto cioccolato* from the busy bar. It's impossible to be in Italy and not have this initiation into the day. The pastry is warm and the espresso strong and sweet. Things are definitely looking up.

Deciding to take in some more of Empoli on this glorious morning, I wander through the car-free *zona pedonale* as folks make their way to work. Small businesses line the pedestrian streets supporting the local economy, not name brands profiting some distant corporate office.

Turning a corner, another piazza opens up with a flowing fountain in its center, a classical statue of the naked female form. Three women sit with their backs to each other holding up a large overflowing dish. Sunlight glints on the water as it falls around them. At each corner below, a lion pours water from its mouth.

The gentle cascade adds its music to the quiet space with hardly anyone around save for a fully-clothed woman opening up her flower shop and some locals passing through. Porticos line three sides. Rows of green shutters above, some half open, let in the morning light. A man calmly strolls out of his shop and lights a cigarette.

The large green-and-white marble facade of the church faces the piazza, its campanile rising up into the clear blue sky. The tolling bell suddenly breaks the silence as a dog barks in concert.

I'm in an Italian dream come to life.

Making my way to the station with a caffeinated spring in my step, I head off to Florence.

Lost in the Renaissance

Walking out of Santa Maria Novella station, I head in a different direction than usual. I love that there's a usual.

The dark and dominating walls of a low-lying fortress, Fortezza da Basso, appear in front of me. While it may be of historical interest, its pointed masonry and defence towers send a clear message: stay away.

Fortunately, at the end of all this medieval protection is a park. Looking out over a large pond with a central fountain, surrounded by greenery in the midst of this busy city, I sit on a bench and study the Florence app on my iPhone.

Florence is overwhelming. You can't possibly see everything in one day, although some of my fellow Americans do try.

What with one historic possibility after another, I decide on a more spontaneous approach. Michelangelo's David is on display at the Accademia up here north of the river and not too far.

Without the aid of a map, I arrive at a piazza with a large wrought-iron indoor market, the Mercato Centrale. Counters of fresh meat, fish, cheeses and other local produce fill the interior as locals do their shopping. There's not a tourist in sight.

Back across the piazza, I continue my search for David, almost tripping in one of the many potholes that appear without warning in Florence.

A sudden blast of air conditioning rushes over me and I turn to see a McDonald's. What on earth is this doing here? Who would want to eat this plastic junk when we're in Florence, in Italy, home of the best food in the world? It's filled with tourists and teenagers.

The cultural and nutritional contrast with the local market is a shocking reality that lingers in my mind.

Finally I arrive at a long line of people stretching round an entire city block. This must be it. But Michelangelo or not, I'm not standing in this heat under the full melting sun.

This is the occasional drawback of spontaneous decisions. If I'd bought a ticket in advance, I could have gone straight in.

Around the far side of the Accademia is a spacious rectangular piazza. I sit and gaze out from under a portico and consider my next move.

Two small fountains stand either side, each with fantastical figures, half sea-creature, half human. At the far end, a ruling Medici no doubt, sits on his high-horse. But whatever history is behind all this, it's the space itself that draws me, how pleasing it is to the eye, to the senses. With no bars or restaurants, its focus is not commercial, it's a place to meet, to gather, to lounge, to just be.

I consult my map to find this is Piazza della Santissima Annunziata, the name of the church at the north end which at this time of day is closed. I still can't decide where to go next. Just thinking about it is too much. I begin to feel a dull, familiar ache inside.

But it's from nothing I've eaten. It's that uncontrollable pang of loss again. By now I've learnt there's no alternative but to just let it happen.

Wandering past the church, I spy some greenery further up, which means a park which means more shade. The Giardino dei Semplici has an entrance fee, but regardless of the cost I need some nature and some peace and quiet. And a nap.

For a botanic garden, it's small and unimpressive but it does the job. I find a bench and lie down.

Gazing up at the trees outlined against clear blue sky, I slowly come to, empty as a child. I've never paid for a nap before.

I consult the map for where else to visit in the remains of my disappearing day. There's a church at the end of the street that looks interesting.

I'm not sure how, but I manage to miss it completely

and end up back in Piazza Annunziata.

What is going on? Is there some kind of joke I'm not getting?

Across the piazza is the Ospedale degli Innocenti, the Orphan's Museum which, according to my guide, includes some artistic treasures. Except it's closed for renovation.

I have to find something.

Inside the loggia of the Ospedale, tucked away at one end, is a barred window. According to the sign below, it was through these bars with just enough space for an infant that women anonymously passed their unwanted babies and was in constant use over four centuries. That's a lot of babies.

Not only that, the building was designed by none other than Brunelleschi, the man responsible for the giant dome of the Duomo. Now I have to come back.

Looking down the main street from the piazza, that giant dome stands waiting for me.

I manage a glimmer of trust that all this lost meandering is meant to be.

Then I remember Italy Unpacked and Giorgio Locatelli's comment on pilgrimage—*"The place you don't know is the place you find yourself."*

I need to write that down or tattoo it on my arm.

The line into the Duomo is long but moving and in fifteen minutes I'm inside.

The Cattedrale di Santa Maria del Fiore, to give it its full title, is a vast space of emptiness without too much to distract from its architectural marvels. Although achieving its goal of making one small, it's plainer, less decorative than I expected, until I look down.

The floor of the Duomo is a masterpiece of tile work covering the entire space with geometric patterns of colored marble, moving the eye as if it's alive.

Following these circular patterns along the central nave, I join everyone else in a collective gaze upward.

A detailed and highly-populated fresco covers the entire concave surface of the dome, depicting the story of the Last Judgment: damnation for sinners and redemption for the faithful. Although that may be factually questionable, the effect is remarkable.

Under my feet, the cupola is mirrored in an illusion of perspective tile work making the floor seem like it's falling into an equally giant bowl.

Now I'm getting sensory overload. And I'm not in the mood to climb to the top of the dome either. I need food.

Working my way back outside, I find a recommended eatery close by, I Fratellini, The Little Brothers, and order a delicious handmade *panino*.

Nourished and re-enabled, I let myself wander with no plan, no destination.

Turning into a quiet side street, a sure way to avoid the crowds, I look up to see a sculpted bust of the Virgin Mary behind framed glass. In a small alleyway, a beautiful framed fresco of the Annunciation sits high up in the corner, easy to miss. On another street corner behind glass is a large framed fresco of the *sacra famiglia*.

Religious images are inescapable in Italy. In the days before electricity and newspapers, art communicated what the spoken word could only suggest. No wonder there's so much of it here.

On a busier street, tall wooden doors open into a dramatically lit corridor. On its walls, mounted sections of decorative stucco are displayed as art pieces. At the far end, a quiet sunlit courtyard of yellow ochre rises three stories; potted palms in front of a double archway hide a parked scooter; a small fountain gurgles from a side wall.

Back on the street, through another corridor, an arch frames another courtyard, its walls covered in frescos, sunlight streaming into the tranquil space.

I start to fantasize about living here, what it would be like to have such a courtyard to come back to every day. But I don't, at least not yet, and right now I haven't the faintest idea where I am, except that it's beautiful.

At the end of the street, a large gray stone arch frames one side of a small piazza. A market stall does fast business selling fresh colorful produce to the locals. I seem to be the only tourist here. Am I really that far out of the way?

By now I'm completely lost, which isn't bad considering I'm in the home of the Renaissance. There's so much to see, I could spend the entire day getting lost. And anyway, what is lost, exactly? Just because you're not following a route, doesn't mean you're not going somewhere or you can't enjoy where you are and be open to something new.

I need to remember that as well. But it's not always easy, especially today, even with a map. And even though I'm enjoying wandering around Florence, something in me prefers the security of knowing where I am and where I'm going.

Through more backstreets, I enter the wide-open space of Piazza di Santa Croce. With no central fountain and all its stone benches in the sun, it's more of a place to pass through, or maybe an evening concert as the sun goes down. In the heat of this afternoon, most folks are standing at the perimeter in the shade.

The giant white, pink and green marble facade of Basilica di Santa Croce overlooks the piazza, the cloaked and brooding figure of Florentine poet Dante standing next to it. I'm tempted to go in and cool down, but I have to be at Silvia's for six o'clock.

I can't believe this has taken me all day.

Getting lost may be one way of exploring, but this has been different. I've been disoriented, out of touch with my inner compass, that connection between the sense of space and the sense of self. It's disconcerting not to be able to feel what I've always relied on.

Disorientation, loss, mourning—I'm still adjusting to being orphaned now both my parents are gone.

Going in what I hope is the right direction, I stop at a *pasticceria* to pick up some dessert for tonight. The berry *torta* in the window looks good.

Maybe they know where a music shop is.

"*Per favore, dov'è un shop di musica?*" I ask the woman behind the counter, playing my best air guitar.

"*Sì, sì!*" comes the reply.

I produce my paper map and point to where we are.

"*Oppozit Casa Medici,*" she tells me in broken English with a smile and a wave of her hand down the street.

With a *grazie mille*, I pay for the pie and head in direction *Casa*. Fortunately, it's on the way to the station.

And yes, the shop is closed. I should have guessed. Sorry Silvia, your strings will have to wait.

The *regionale* back to Empoli has no air-conditioning. It's stuffy and hot and just about bearable with one or two of the small tilted windows open.

Getting off the train, the cool evening breeze brings me back to some sense of normal and I walk to Silvia's, route memorized. At least there's one place I know how to get to.

The front door buzzes open and I go upstairs and wait at the kitchen table.

Silvia comes in with a brief smile, sees the dessert I bought and says, sharply, to stop buying gifts for them. I'm a bit taken aback and pass some comments to smooth the situation, but I can tell something's going on. Is it because the *torta* equals kilos? Is it because she doesn't want me to feel obliged? Or is it because she just doesn't like pie?

She mentions a friend is coming over tomorrow night for dinner and I suggest she use the dessert then instead.

This makes it okay and we continue our evening, feathers unruffled.

Watching her smoke a cigarette on the balcony, it's clear Silvia is a little stressed. Maybe something happened at school today.

Sitting down to dinner with her and her girls, we manage to connect a lot more and the mood lightens considerably.

Silvia is a combination of beauty, wit and smolder, and even though that smolder caught fire earlier, I enjoy her company immensely. The whole experience is an education in being Italian.

Driving into the darkness of the countryside, she drops me off once more at the villa.

Standing alone in the quiet space, I take a deep breath, the faint musty smell a welcome return to rural life after the hot and busy streets of Florence.

I feel so blessed for another night in this villa in Tuscany. Thank you, Silvia. How can I ever repay you?

Waking up to the sound of the birds and the magical golden light is a moment I want to stay in for the rest of my life.

I get up and shower, take some breakfast and step outside in the cool morning shade to write.

Finding the
Moment

After an enjoyable train ride from Empoli, I arrive in Pisa only to be accosted by urban life. It's hot and dirty and full of tourists and hawkers and I don't really want to be here, but I'm in between trains with time to explore.

Sidewalk cafes tempt me in the shade of porticos. I walk past a table of men in animated discussion, clearly about something of great importance, which means it could be anything really—a football player, a politician, the quality of the food, the bitterness of the coffee, how to iron a shirt. The list is endless, for everything is important in Italy.

Quickly tired of the row of commercial branding down the long pedestrian shopping street that extends to the Arno, I turn through a covered alley into the quiet calm of an almost-empty piazza. A child's laughter fills the air as a ball bounces along, tiny steps in pursuit.

I sit on a bench under a tree and take a moment.

These public spaces, the meeting place of Italian life, invite not just connection but reflection. As I'm the only one here apart from a couple at the far end and the little girl with her mother, I sit undisturbed. No hawkers, no harassment, just empty space and the occasional cyclist passing through.

I need these moments, this moment.

Something in me starts to let go, something old and tight. The longer I sit, the more I notice it, that clinging childhood desire for maternal security. Even though I only really needed it in my early years, it's been a theme in my life ever since. It's as if I'm constantly learning to become a man, whatever that is.

Just knowing she was alive was a subconscious security. Now she has really gone, it's up to me to depend not just on my own wits, but on a greater power around me, within me.

Through an archway to another quieter street, tall porticos offer more shade and coffee, another welcome break in this busy town. I'm starting to relax. I'm even starting to like being here.

Over the river, away from the crowds, I enter another quiet piazza, across which stands the University building. Its top layer of plaster has been scratched into designs exposing the darker layers beneath, a technique called *sgraffiti* I've seen on other facades in Florence—the same stucco that was on display in that corridor.

These decorated buildings make for such a harmonious sight. Now *sgraffiti* has become graffiti, that harmony has exploded into a spray-painted statement of anger and objection.

Have we lost touch with beauty? That being in the eye of the beholder, it makes me ponder the question even more—have we lost touch with our own?

A horse and buggy, its driver with whip in hand, stands in front of the steps up to the entrance waiting for customers. I contemplate a ride but continue on foot.

Pisa has the one piece of architecture whose world-renowned fame is due to subsidence—the Leaning Tower. Tickets are €38 for the Tower, the Duomo, the Baptistery and... hold on—thirty-eight euros? I could buy dinner with that and have some change. For a traveler on a budget, that's not just unfair, that's criminal.

Walking around the Campo dei Miracoli, the Field of Miracles, although it's more like the Field of Tourists, I gaze at the magnificence of the architecture around me, an appreciative if reluctant outsider.

The Leaning Tower is dangerously leaning, an upward, angular spiral of vertigo that wants to fall over but doesn't. The Fontana dei Putti, its three giant stone babies holding up the crest of the city, stand triumphant, replicated along with the tower on shopping bags the world over.

I take a few photos and head out of the trap. Besides, I have a train waiting to take me somewhere I've been longing to return ever since I left last year.

Escape into Lucca

Across the street from the station, the other side of a wide grass area stretching in either direction, is the wall. This long brick boundary that defines the old city of Lucca is the border between one world and another. As I get closer, it becomes bigger and bigger until I feel a dwarf next to it. Through a dimly-lit passageway and up some steps, I emerge on top of the wall to survey the haven of shade and tranquility before me.

Lined for much of the way by an avenue of trees, the wall has a wide path for cyclists, joggers and pedestrians to circumnavigate the city or just sit and enjoy the view.

Descending a ramp into this flat *comune* of yellow ochre hues, I feel myself relax into its languid vibe. People stroll without the striding intent of actually going somewhere. Others glide by on two wheels, occasionally pedaling. Lucca is not a place to hurry.

In true Italian style, a policeman and woman leisurely patrol the streets in their Valentino-designed uniforms, he with stubble and designer shades, she in heeled shoes and earrings, her hair falling loose under her cap. I look around for a red carpet, then with a smile remember the entire town, the entire country is a red carpet.

Opening out into Piazza Napoleone, known by the locals as Piazza Grande, probably to downplay the old French rule, the vast space is even more noticeable by the lack of people. Everyone is in the shade of this tree-lined piazza sipping chianti, chatting over coffee, smoking or just hanging out. A central statue of a noblewoman holding a staff, a naked youth by her side, overlooks us all as if giving her approval.

Turning a corner, the familiar face of Mark Knopfler adorns a poster for the Lucca Summer Festival coming up in July, just as he did last year. The operatic strains of an accordion waft through the air, the aria providing the perfect serenade to the home of Giacomo Puccini.

Music, it seems, is a fabric of life in Lucca.

Piazza San Michele, although smaller than Piazza Grande, is the central point of the city, dominated by the white marble church of San Michele in Foro, although it's more of a weathered dirty-white marble with water stains, meaning character and history.

The icon of the divine feminine, the Madonna holding her child, stands on a corner of the church, shafts of golden light struck in brass emanating around her. From the top of the church, Archangel Michael poses high above the piazza, protecting the city.

Lucca is known as the City of a Hundred Churches. Actually there are ninety-nine, but that just doesn't have the same ring about it.

Wandering further, I look up, always a good habit in new cities as long as you don't trip over, to find a stunning gold mosaic under the eve of a church—Christ giving his blessing, an angel either side with the twelve disciples below. Even for a non-religious man like me, it's a potent, beautiful image.

A block away through an arched passage is the protected space of Piazza dell'Anfiteatro.

This oval-shaped piazza, possibly the most famous part of the city, has no church or fountain. Built on the remains of a small Roman amphitheater, colorful four and five-story residences enclose its perimeter with shops, restaurants and bars at ground level. People sit at outdoor tables sipping *caffè*. Like the rest of Lucca, it's a chilled-out scene.

It's the beginning of May so the busy season hasn't started, yet standing in front of me is a tour group. But there's no loud, frantic activity, no flags, no umbrellas, just a small group of folks and their guide milling around, taking their time about it. They fit right in.

Across the piazza, a young couple take a long kiss. What better way to show the tourists what Italy is really about.

Finding a spot to sit, I breathe in the relaxed life of the piazza and start to feel replenished after hours on my feet.

Finally exiting through one of the four passages at each quadrant, I stop and stare. Opposite a flower shop, a lone street performer sits cross-legged in a monk's robe, the hood pulled far over his head, floating above the ground. Literally.

Of course it's a trick, but it's so well done and the first time I'm seeing it that I have to give him some money. Only later will I find out how, which ruins the magic. Maybe I can forget. Wouldn't that be a trick, to consciously forget? I'll have to wait for old age to do that, whenever that is.

Back in Piazza Grande, a colorful carousel carries happy children in its orbit as proud parents look on. Lucca really is a peaceful place.

On my way to the station, I pass the guitar shop I stopped in last year and buy strings for Silvia.

Leaving
la Villa

Last night was the last supper for a while with Silvia and her girls. I got to restring her guitar and play for her again. In that moment she was my muse, the instrument alive with creative fire, the power of the feminine stirring my invention, just as she has for countless artists down the centuries. I haven't played like that in a while.

But now it's time to shower and pack. This is my last morning at the villa and I have to pull up my portable roots. Having had such profound moments here, it's not the easiest thing to do, but it's part of life on the road.

Silvia comes racing up the drive. She's looking sharp in her leather jacket, her long dark hair braided back. She means business.

As we drive to the station, it's clear she's had a busy morning already. It's been a crazy week for her and having me around has somehow made it a mixture of pleasant distraction and added pressure. I look forward to another time when we can relax and connect a little more.

With an *arrivederci* and an air-kiss on each cheek, Silvia zooms back into her life.

Inside the station, the familiar voice of the red Trenitalia ticket machine broadcasts her endearing Italian accent.

"Be-ware of peek pockets," she warns, for any pickpockets to hear.

Ticket in hand, I wrestle my bags down the steps to the *sottopassaggio* and up again to platform five.

Seeing the small oval green-and-yellow box, I am reminded to validate my ticket—a crucial step in Italian public transport, which if forgotten can lead to a hefty fine.

The sound of the hole being punched and the printer running the date and time, done in two seconds, is another familiarity of Italian travel. It may be a small thing, but its meaning is far greater. It signals the readiness for departure, the excitement of the journey ahead.

Finding some shade, I wait for the train to Poggibonsi to meet my dear English friend, Sophie, whom I first met at that cafe in Siena last year.

On the forty-minute ride, she texts me she's running late. No problem. Since when has anybody been on time in Italy?

Country
Life

In the slightly grubby bar at Poggibonsi station, I order a *panino*, grilled *per favore*. It comes back sad, soft and microwaved as my culinary expectations wither and die in front of me. I pay for an *acqua naturale* and sit down. *Naturale* means still water. I break it open and *fzzzzz*—it's *frizzante*, carbonated.

It's another moment of understanding that expectations are meaningless in this country, even if requests, labels, signs and directions are clearly stated. It also means that as I'm a tourist, some Italian barkeepers don't give a monkey's what I want.

I eat and drink because I need to. It's a sullen appeasement that reminds me yet again that the legendary food of Italy is not always guaranteed. In a station bar it's non-existent.

Some local men sit at an outside table with an air of

danger, as if waiting for trouble is a daily pastime. Sophie pulls up in her Land Rover, waving, as the men watch our every move. I throw in my bags and we drive off, escaping the delights of Poggibonsi station.

It's been four months since I stayed with her in London and we have much to catch up on. The drive through the countryside goes by in a blur of conversation.

Sophie is a personal chef and rarely has time off, so I'm both lucky and happy she can spend time with me. I have enjoyed her company since the moment we met. She has a remarkable quality that encourages respect and a loving attitude just by being herself.

Four kilometers down a bumpy dirt track we pull into the gates of an old Tuscan villa shrouded in trees, its weathered stucco walls draped in ivy. Now split into apartments, hers is upstairs.

Paco, her *cane corso,* a giant of a pure-bred dog since Roman times and as good-natured as she is, rises from his bed to greet us.

As I've come to learn, they're inseparable. The more I see them together, the more it seems they've known each other long before they were dog and human.

The apartment has that uniquely rustic Tuscan style—terracotta floors, wood-beamed ceilings, an open-plan kitchen and living room with a wrought-iron circular stair leading up to a mezzanine loft where I will be camped.

The view from the window overlooks gently rolling countryside, cumulus billowing in the wide open sky.

After wrestling my bags up the tight staircase, Sophie suggests we take a walk to show me the area and introduce me to some old friends of hers, Gianni and Paola. Paco has to stay behind, though. It's too far for his stiff joints, poor boy.

Down a long track past a working farm, we arrive at a small one-story house. Two lively young dogs welcome us, vying for attention. Gianni comes out and picks them up in one big love-bundle providing a point of participation in their country life.

As is the tradition in Italy, guests are offered coffee and before long Paola has brewed up their well-used flame-scorched *moka*.

Neither Gianni nor Paola speak much English, but that's okay. There are so many ways to communicate in a foreign country with gestures, body language, emotional tone and eye contact, being fluent in another language is not strictly necessary. We can get a point across. And if we're stuck, Sophie is translator in her impeccable Italian from having been here for so many years.

In our half-Italian, half-English, we get along instantly.

The dogs play-fight under the kitchen table, growling, knocking our legs in their constant tumble.

Agreeing to meet up with them again while I'm here, Sophie and I make our way back to the villa.

Two newborn lambs lie by the side of the track, abandoned as the herd wanders across a field. Maybe this is their mother's strategy to build character and survival skills. A little early, though.

Sophie carefully picks them up and we take them to the farm. Whether they will reunite with their irresponsible mother or end up on the dinner table, I cannot say.

Stopped in my Tracks

The next morning, Sophie drops me off in the local town of Colle di Val d'Elsa, spoken without the "di" but mostly shortened to just Colle. More precisely, she's taking me to Colle Alta, the upper, older part of town.

Approaching what looks like a castle, we drive through the arch of Porta Nova and down medieval streets steeped in history, some barely wide enough for the car. She lets me out at the bottom of some steps and tells me to walk up and then down as far as I can and take the lift.

Lift?

Sophie drives off with a wave as I begin my stroll amongst the deep terracotta, the history, the atmosphere, the light—I'm in Italian heaven again.

Walking past some steps leading down through an archway, something stops me in my tracks.

Singing.

I go down, the sound becoming louder with every step. This is not a recording. As I enter the cool of this underground chapel, a chorus of male voices fills the space, hidden behind a screen in an alcove, singing to God. I sit in a pew and gaze at the simple frescos adorning the arches above, the mix of art and music transporting me. Closing my eyes, I let the voices wash over me in their calm, uplifting cadence, the call and response of Gregorian chant.

Suddenly, a peal of church bells overwhelms the chorus, blending in their cacophony. Back outside, I watch the bells swing in their tower. It's a deafening, wonderful sight. It's also noon.

As instructed, I wander down the cobblestoned hill as far as I can. Rounding a corner, the hill opens up into a piazza overlooking the panorama of terracotta roofs and tiny streets. Seeing a woman enter a steel-and-glass box in the middle of this *belvedere*, I realize this is the lift. It looks so modern, so out of place, but highly useful, taking me down to a deep *sottopassaggio* leading out to the streets below.

Old men in caps stand together in the central piazza talking about the latest goings-on as is their morning tradition, one not to be broken. Tradition is deeply woven into everyday life in Italy and is kept alive by each succeeding generation. Women shop in market stalls as they have done for centuries; boys laugh, pushing each other, young hopefuls attracting attention; a young woman sits reading a book, sipping *caffè* in the shade of a portico, ignoring an admirer passing by. She's used to it.

Absorbing Italian life, I stop and sit and listen—voices, laughter, birds, an occasional scooter, but no constant traffic. I love this about small towns.

Italy is unique. Of course, you can find people all over the world doing the same things, but the way they do it here, the places they do it in, the atmosphere—there's no other country like it. Whatever happens, whatever chaos goes on in this crazy place, even the bad things that happen, the passion of its people will always endure, there's always tomorrow, life will always be here, and that life is beautiful.

Tourists, Towers and Torture

Breakfast with Sophie is a high-energy start to the day. We begin with strong *caffè*, of course, and some cool tunes. Not one to idle, she doesn't sit around and chat, but jumps straight into preparing food for her cooking gig tonight and I, more of the idler, change tack and muck in.

In the midst of chopping carrots, she gets a call that a potential buyer is on his way to look at the apartment, so I make myself scarce with a long walk and some context.

Halfway down the track, the dogs start barking. There must be at least five of them, big white *maremmani* sheepdogs, snarling, fangs bared and I am so glad they are behind a fence. These dogs would rip me apart.

The loud voice of a man slowly shuts them up as I continue my walk in peace.

One idyllic vista after another, I take in the Tuscan countryside on this glorious morning. After an hour's loop,

I come to an empty villa behind Sophie's house.

The villa is a magnificent, sprawling stone shell waiting for someone to buy it and turn it into the place it wants to become and maybe once was. With a panoramic view across the hills of Tuscany, it's a shame it's been empty for so long.

I sit on some steps in the shade. It's so quiet here, the silence amplifying the sound of bees. There must be a hive close by. Even in the shade, it's still hot.

I close my eyes and with a deep breath, drop into stillness, the hypnotic rhythm of the bees taking me deeper until I find myself in an extended moment of no thought, no time.

I don't know how long I was sitting on those steps, but something in me said it's time to return.

Back at the house, the visitor has come and gone and Sophie tells me Gianni called. He wants to take me somewhere and I'm not about to say no.

Hiking out to their place again, Gianni and Paola give me a warm welcome. These people are so down-to-earth, honest and real.

Gianni is a man's man and a year younger than me, although he smokes two packs a day and looks a bit older. Paola makes us coffee while Gianni and I sit and have some laughs, which go something like this:

"Who is Giuseppe Verdi?" I ask.

"Joe Green," comes the reply.

"Antonio Vivaldi?"

"Tony Highlife."

"Niccolò Paganini?"

"Nick the Tiny Pagan."

"Giacomo Puccini?"

"Jack the Dipper."

"Luciano Pavarotti?"

"Lou the Broken Floor Tile."

"How about the architect, Palladio?"

"God's Balls!"

By now we are in hysterics, Gianni hacking up a piece of lung while I wipe the tears from my face. Paola looks up from the kitchen, managing a smile at the boys' humor.

All this laughter is such a welcome change from my months of seriousness. I had forgotten it was even possible.

Coffee downed, it's time to go.

Driving through prime Tuscan countryside, past olive groves and vineyards, we end up at the top of a hill and through the gates of Pasolini's Organic Farm.

We are welcomed by a fresh-faced young girl about eighteen years old, a natural beauty without any makeup or city glamour. She doesn't need it. Two boys the same age appear and they, too, are the picture of health, ripe young men who look like they've stepped out of an issue of GQ. Yet more examples of the handsome Italian gene pool.

Luciano Pasolini is a high school friend of Gianni and they joke together in that uniquely masculine way, backslapping, shoving and laughing heartily.

Inside the production plant, they can their own fruit and vegetables and bottle the juice. It's not often I get to see the machinery of a local organic farm and it reminds me of how the small local producer is a feature of Tuscan life, their goods exported to the rest of Italy and sometimes beyond.

I mention to Luciano I live nearby San Francisco, and he comments that's where the pioneering ideas start and then spread over the world. He has a point. It was the epicenter of the '60s counterculture, spawning the Whole Earth Catalog as but one example.

I buy some organic pear juice for Sophie and with hearty goodbyes, we head off to our next destination.

San Gimignano is a medieval hilltop town full of tall towers, each one successively built to dominate the other, Gianni informs me, as depictions of Italian male virility.

We pass the local Torture Museum and I decide to take a closer, morbid look.

One exhibit is a skeleton in a cage, the victim locked up inside and starved to death. Another wax figure models an H-shaped sharpened iron cross, the bottom blades piercing the throat either side of the windpipe, the top blades piercing the underside of the jaw and into the tongue. Any movement would result in extreme and agonizing pain. It was used by the Inquisition for heretics and unbelievers to repent their evil ways before their execution or, if they were lucky, live to abide by the rules of the Catholic Church. And this was an instrument of religious faith?

I can't stay here a moment longer.

Uphill, past more tourist shops selling the traditional hand-painted *maiolica* pottery, a pleasant distraction from torture, past a stuffed wild boar in front of a *salumeria,* we turn into an empty side street.

Through a studded wooden door, part of a much larger wooden door big enough for a coach and horses, we enter a hidden courtyard.

An ancient well stands under an arch; two large bells stand mute in a corner; steps lead up to an open passageway. Every wall has frescos or sculpted reliefs designed into them as if they were built to display them, the heraldry and allegories of justice clearly part of the town's civic history.

It's hard to believe we're the only ones here. This is the perk of being with a local. Gianni is clearly proud of being able to show me this secret of San Gimignano.

Back outside, across Piazza del Duomo, a cavernous space framed by a huge arch is the meeting place for the over-fifty. Sitting on the stonework and a row of chairs across the center, they discuss the matters of the day and watch the evening's *passeggiata*, when folks come out for their sunset stroll. It's yet another example of how community and connection are so important in Italian life.

Down in the adjoining Piazza della Cisterna, some

loud Americans disturb the calm, so out of place as if they're visiting a zoo.

"Oh look, Frank! Isn't that *quaint!*"

No wonder patience wears thin with the locals.

Dondoli's proclaims itself Gelato World Champion four years in a row. Having already had some of the world's best gelato elsewhere, I'm not buying this tourist gimmick. Just to make the point, they have it printed in four languages.

Crossing the piazza, the other side of the *cisterna*, the large central well that descends into a water tank, Gianni and I take a seat at the outdoor tables of La Terrazza for an *aperitivo*. A glass of pinot grigio for him while I order my favorite, *affogato*—espresso poured over vanilla gelato. Decadent and delicious.

As we connect in our hybrid English and Italian, it turns out Gianni studied literature at the University of Milan. I would never have guessed. It's so important not to judge people by first impressions. Everyone has a history worth investigating. I like him.

After another glorious drive through rolling Tuscan hills in the evening sun, I bid Gianni and Paola *arrivederci* and walk back to the villa.

Rolling
Thunder

It's Sunday morning and this time, breakfast with Sophie is a more relaxed affair.

As much as we get along, I don't want to overstay my welcome, and having little or no internet is making it difficult to plan my travels.

All this amounts to feeling displaced and insecure again, not knowing where I'll be on Tuesday. But that's part of my Grand Couchsurfing Tour of Italy—dive in and see what happens. From there, things just show up in that magical way that happens on the road.

Why do I forget that?

Rolling thunder deafens the house. I run outside to record the heavenly drama on my iPhone while Sophie prepares for her next cooking job. Sitting under the massive oak tree in the courtyard, I use this elemental time to contemplate the past few months.

It all started when my mother began her demise back in the snow and cold of England. Ever since she died a few weeks later, my slate got wiped clean. The identity of the designer, musician, filmmaker, screenwriter—they've all gone. Regardless of the powerful connection to family in Denmark, of returning to my beloved Italy, I still feel in some kind of limbo.

Now I'm moving from place to place, absorbing, collecting experience on a pilgrimage into the unknown.

The words of the father from Novalesa stay with me: *a pilgrimage is a journey you make on your own to face the challenges that bring you closer to God.*

I've always had a problem with the word God. There's just too much baggage—dogma, guilt, punishment and violence to name a few. Yet I feel the presence of an infinite and benevolent intelligence surrounding me and even within me.

Many times I feel the discomfort of not knowing my place in the world, yet something pulls me onward. Whatever I'm meant to find is not obvious.

Some people I can relate to, others I cannot. It's a strange space where I'm not sure who I am anymore. I'm becoming so much older, a wandering soul with no home, no real ground of my own.

I wonder how much I'm perpetuating it, how much I'm not getting back on purpose, back in gear. Yes, that's it. Take charge. Be a man.

That certainly would be the expected answer.

But I'm not the man I was before. I've been initiated into my elder years where that drive doesn't matter as much, at least not in the way that it did. It's more about collaborating with the hidden energies of life, about trust and faith. It's deeper, more potent, more fulfilling.

This isn't about my mother anymore. Her death was the catalyst for something else entirely.

A refreshing calm descends as thunder rumbles off in the distance.

"Tea?" Sophie asks with her bright smile, leaning over the balcony.

Over the
Arno

After the continued silence of the Couchsurfing hosts I applied to in Florence, my hopes have all but disappeared and my worries taken center stage. This is not a good sign.

Just when I thought I might have to rough it under a bridge or worse, book a hotel room, there comes a light in the darkness and her name is Judith. She just confirmed being my host for tonight two blocks south of the river in Oltrarno.

This last-minute brinksmanship is something to savor as it's part of Couchsurfing, part of the adventure. The security of advanced booking may appeal to the majority, and to me of late, but this by-the-seat-of-your-pants travel is a lot more exciting. It's good for me.

Bags packed, I'm ready to leave.

The bus to Florence leaves from Colle and Sophie has offered to drive me to the stop. On the way, we talk about our plans and where we can meet up next. As she regularly visits family in England, no doubt we'll find somewhere.

She pulls up to the curb and I haul my bags out of the car. With a hug and a wave, I bid Sophie *a presto*. It's been such a joy to stay with her, even though space was tight. Maybe next time will be under more spacious circumstances. I hope so.

Using my best *italiano*, I buy a one-way ticket to Florence from the very polite uniformed woman behind the counter of the tourist office.

The bus is delayed, or more endearingly, 'retarded' in the literal translation, so there's a bit of waiting, not that I mind. It's practice.

Finally, the retarded bus arrives. The driver sits behind the wheel while I wonder where to put my bag. Am I supposed to open the luggage door? He's not moving, so I assume so.

It's not the easiest door to open and jams behind the passenger door with a loud 'clack'. Bad design. They could have made some clearance. But this is an Italian bus and Italy is all about clash and chaos and connection.

The driver comes out yelling, pulls the door free, kicks my bag into the hold and continues his rant while he climbs back into the cab. I find a seat and we drive off at an angry speed with more cursing and ranting until eventually he runs out of steam and we have a peaceful ride to Florence.

Maybe I helped him vent something deep in his

troubled bus-driver soul. Maybe he won't go home tonight and yell at his wife. Maybe I saved her from a beating. The Universe works in mysterious ways.

Getting off the bus at Santa Maria Novella bus station, I walk to the adjacent Santa Maria Novella train station, drop my bags at the *deposito bagagli* once more and walk into town. I've got an hour or two before I meet Judith.

There's surprisingly less people here during May. Compared with the September crowds last year, Florence feels more civilized. There's more physical space to take it all in.

I'd hoped for more connection to Italy in one of its most famous cities, but it's becoming another strange day. The thrill of adventure has evaporated and I'm feeling lost again, displaced with no real plan. Gone is that powerful sense of returning, of belonging.

What happened?

I know what happened. I'd just rather not deal with it, thank you very much.

I end up at the Strozzi for lunch, its elegant inner courtyard providing the ambience I need, considering my state of mind.

Two artists assemble an installation in the center space. A slender tree trunk is suspended with its spindly roots above a floating tile platform a foot from the floor, a contrast of the natural world with the artificial.

I feel just as uprooted.

After tasty but overpriced *pranzo*, I finally buy a ticket

for the Springtime in the Renaissance exhibition to see if that will shift my mood as well as educate me.

Seeing these Renaissance statues in a gallery is just not the same as seeing them where they were meant to be. They've become abstract. They've lost their context. I deem it a waste of money and continue my mood outside on the street.

I'm in a funk in Florence. That of itself is an anomaly. Being in Italy in a bad mood shouldn't exist in the same sentence. Or maybe I'm learning to be Italian.

Wandering past oversized pots of geraniums on Via Tornabuoni, one of the main shopping streets, I see some familiar sights—the Column of Justice weighing her scales of truth; the statues of the seasons on Ponte Santa Trinità.

Crossing the bridge, I look out over the Arno and decide to take a stroll along its banks. Sun glints on the water as a lone oarsman rows his way upriver. With a deep exhale, I begin to lighten up.

I'm in Florence walking along the Arno. Life really isn't that bad.

As I make my way further into Oltrarno, Piazza del Carmine opens up before me, the very place that eluded me last week. It's not the most romantic piazza in the world with a parking lot at one end, no central fountain and no people. Maybe that's why I couldn't find it.

The decorative facade of Santa Maria del Carmine has gone, revealing its rough-hewn building underneath. It's also closed, as is the Brancacci Chapel next door, which

I've heard has some beautiful frescos.

I begin to see this as a metaphor: I'm not in the most romantic mood, dark thoughts are parked at one end of my mind and I have no central overflowing happiness, at least none that is obvious. I'm all alone. My happy facade has gone revealing my rough-hewn troubled self beneath. My church is closed, hiding the treasures of my soul.

I should write poetry.

Crossing Ponte Vespucci, I make my way back to the station, buying a cake for Judith on the way.

The Dinner Party

I watch the meter increase as my taxi sits in rush-hour traffic.

€12 later, Judith buzzes me in and I drag my beast-of-a-bag up two flights of steep, tight Oltrarno stairs.

"Hello. My, you're tall," Judith observes as she opens her old wooden front door.

I stoop through the low doorway, narrowly missing my head on the lintel, to find Judith's apartment filled with character. Not just old, but historical, its original wood-beamed ceilings intact. Dark inlaid furniture and oriental rugs give it a distinctly bohemian feel; framed black-and-white photos of her ancestors cover one wall of the hallway.

The study doubles as a guest room. Larger than a closet but smaller than half a bedroom, I can just fit myself and my bags and stretch out on the camping bed she's set up for me. That's all I need. It's part of the adventure. Besides, I love being surrounded by books.

Snapshots of a passing conversation drift into this cozy space from the open window facing the street below. I'm going to like staying here.

Connecting in the living room over fresh mint-leaf tea and small slices of the dense fruit cake I presented, we have a lot to talk about, from Couchsurfing to cultural mores to local politics and it's clear she knows how to hold a conversation. Well educated, she's a Chicago transplant who's been here for more than thirty years.

Tonight, she's invited me to join her at a garden party.

I change into something more dapper and we take a short walk around the block to get there.

In the garden, a lively group surrounds the *aperitivi,* a mix of English and American ladies with two men, a Brazilian and an American. Introductions are had and more conversations ensue.

As the temperature declines, we migrate inside to find dinner laid out, buffet style. It's easier to mix while standing around and I strike up a conversation with a tall attractive dark-haired American with a great energy, two kids and her husband is across the room.

She's got a natural vibe and we get on like a house on fire. Three alarm. We talk about life, the Universe and everything and end up on Alzheimer's. It's good to talk about deeper topics and I'm happy I can bring up my mother's death with her. It's helping.

The Brazilian, a well spoken, sensitive man with a disarming smile and clear eyes, joins the conversation and offers keen insights into what happens when the mind goes. It turns out he works with hospice patients.

I notice we have backed the tall American into a corner of the kitchen while the party is in the rest of the open-plan dining room. I back off a little to give her some space, but she's happily put. Another woman comes over and physically tries to pull her away, but she wants to stay. I sense her enjoying the attention of two men, neither of whom is her husband. Some kind of statement, perhaps?

He comes over and takes the last of the dessert without offering her any. She makes a comment, but "you missed," is the snide retort. No wonder she wants to stay in the corner with two other men.

It's time for more food and I break the conversation to see Judith sitting alone. I go over to sit with her and we discuss more of our shared love of travel, arriving at India and meditation. I feel her genuine interest in the deeper aspects of life, a realm I previously thought confined to 'spiritual' people. It's only since I've been traveling I've found some of the deepest conversations and connections I've had have been with so-called 'normal' people.

That alone has had a profound effect on the way I interact. Even though I've spent much of my life on a spiritual path, I've stopped referring to myself as spiritual. That's just another box to fit in, another ego trip.

Finally, the tall American comes over to join us.

Americans sit on one side of the room, Brits on the other. I'm with the Americans with a mixed sense of loyalty.

There's all kinds of stories going on, including the mole on someone's pubic area that the doctor was examining up close when his assistant walked in. Such is the stuff of parties in other countries.

I realize I'm feeling better than I have all day—and how much I need people. Being alone and ungrounded has been tough, even though I sense it's been a necessary test of my resolve. Meeting Judith and being at the party tonight has been such a shift of energy. I feel relaxed, grateful and even happy.

It's a reminder that my mood can change in an instant. Just because I've been going through feelings of loss doesn't mean I can't enjoy myself.

The party begins to break up and people make their rounds to say goodbye. The tall American's husband is on a bicycle, whereas she is walking. It's late. He doesn't escort her back or call for a cab. In fact, he wears a grin as he tells her she has to walk alone in the dark through Florence.

I detect all is not well in the family camp. He takes off and she comes over to say goodbye. Looking me squarely in the eyes, she kisses me on each cheek, not casually, but firmly on my skin as if to tell me, 'I'm dying in my relationship, please rescue me.' It's a deep, communicative moment and my soul hears her pleading.

Oh, what human life we have created, the bonds and contracts, the stories and dramas all weaving their web of relationships.

As much as I want to respond, it's not as if I can help her, not in my state and not with my lifestyle. But maybe that's just my excuse.

Later, Judith tells me they are divorced but *separazione in casa*—still living together for the sake of the children. All becomes clear.

Fertile
Fiesole

After a stimulating breakfast with Judith disseminating last night's social adventure, it's time for me to pack and leave. Partly due to our shared generation, she has been a thoroughly engaging host, if only for one night. I have the feeling I'll get to stay with her again.

Just as Judith was a ray of light in the unresponsive world of Florentine hosts, and just when I had written off the middle-aged Italian males of Couchsurfing as a bunch of desperate old men, along comes Marco who just accepted my request.

After confirming my stay with him, I hike up to the station to drop my bags only to return again south of the river. It's calling me.

Crossing back over the Arno, I go through the massive arch of Porta San Frediano, another of the old fortified entrances into the city, its thick studded wooden gates now permanently open for traffic.

Part of the old city wall still stands, topped with battlements, extending from the gate to the river with a tower in the middle. Two women stand chatting, framed inside an archway like a scene from a medieval painting.

Across a busy street at the end of the wall is a large fresco behind glass. Except the glass is so dirty you can't make anything out and the metal grill in front makes it more impossible still. What's the point in such protection if no one can see the beauty behind it?

I know some people like that.

It's only a few blocks to Santa Maria del Carmine and at this time of day, it's open. After yesterday's disappointment, I can finally go in.

The outside may be unfinished, but inside is another matter. High above me, the massive fresco adorning the ceiling is an explosion of pink, blue and gold depicting Christ ascending. It really does seem the sky extends up to heaven. Chandeliers suspended from endless wires shed a golden glow into the space. The Catholic church really knows how to do drama.

At the far end to the right of the altar, I see the famous Brancacci chapel I have to pay for next door. As it's part of the church, it's open and visible, just not up close. From over here behind a rope I can see every surface is covered in frescos. It's been dubbed the Sistine Chapel of Florence. I'd go in if it wasn't filled with tourists.

In no mood for crowds, I return to leafy Piazza Santo

Spirito and sit on a bench in the shade. All this art and beauty can be overwhelming. But that's yet another purpose of the piazza, to stop and digest.

Speaking of which, I'm about ready for lunch.

A few blocks away, a small chalkboard outside Vivanda Gastronomia advertises today's special: *Crostini Neri e Zucchini, Pappa al pomodoro, Caffè,* all organic and all for €10. I'm not going to pass that up.

The grilled zucchini on dark rye *crostini* are smooth and delicious, but it's the *pappa al pomodoro* that hits the spot. This hearty Tuscan bread and tomato soup I first had with Silvia last year. It's been a favorite ever since.

Ending with an espresso, I pay the *conto* and head back to the station and the *deposito bagagli.*

Bags in tow, I board the 1B bus as directed and make my way to Marco's.

Hauling the Beast up yet more flights of steps, I am greeted by a tall, good-looking silver-haired Italian in his sixties. So good looking, he's even done some modeling work he tells me—there's that Italian gene pool again.

This time, I don't get my own room or a bed but the actual couch. It's not often this happens, but I don't mind. It reminds me of my youth.

The high ceilings of his spacious apartment make it even more so. It's a common feature at homes in Italy, giving a sense of grandeur, even in an apartment. Dark polished wood-and-glass double doors open to a large tiled balcony filled with plants wet from last night's rain.

Marco exudes charisma and I can tell he's a ladies man, something I imagine all Italian men aspire to and considering their reputation, frequently succeed. It's a stature he affirms proudly. In fact, most of his Couchsurfing guests are young women. I'm the exception and I'm honored he could fit me into his busy schedule.

After connecting over *caffè* about our shared passions for photography and travel, Marco asks if I want to ride up to the hills overlooking Flo, as the locals call it, on the back of his *motorino*.

Hell, yeah.

It's a smooth, fast ride and I still have to learn to ride pillion and not counterbalance myself on the curves, an instinctive reaction based on speed, gravity and fear. It's also about trusting the driver and the laws of physics, neither of which really matter when you feel you're about to fall off the back and die.

Riding into Fiesole, we find a spot to park. A young American tourist stands outside a bus screaming at an inspector. She didn't validate her ticket, a common mistake amongst visitors and one for which there is no leniency. €50 is an expensive bus ride.

Avoiding the fracas, we enter the Museo Archeologico.

Skeletal remains in a burial chamber make for a mortal reminder lest we think this isn't going to end one day.

Rows of red-and-black Etruscan pottery fill one of the rooms. One large pot in particular catches me eye. A pipe-playing Pan with long beard and tail, in side view, parades his blood-filled member to a group of women, presumably a fertility blessing or just showing off.

It's refreshing to see this pre-Christian image where sex and the human body have such freedom from the myth of sin and two-faced religious morality.

Outside are yet more treasures—an amphitheater and ruins of an Etruscan villa, complete with its own temple.

Grand arches outline a bathing area for hot, lukewarm and cold plunges. They had heating, drains and everything you'd expect from a civil society, in some ways more advanced than developed countries three thousand years later.

They also had an altar for child sacrifice.

This chilling fact puts things into perspective, if only for a moment. Then I think of the amount of children killed in the current wars around the globe, children we never see or read about, anonymous 'casualties' in the news media.

Kill one child for human sacrifice and it's barbarism at its worst. Kill a thousand during wartime and it's collateral damage.

Amidst the ruins are placed modern sculptures of extremely rotund, black naked women rolling in the grass, a distraction from the truth of the temple. As if to say, 'Don't worry, there are enough fat, fertile females to continue the population. What's a few sacrificed children in the bigger scheme of things?'

The amphitheater, Teatro Romano, is used for

concerts. A crew is busy setting up for the evening's performance. I can't wait to see a show here one warm summer night.

Leaving the ruins, Marco and I ride further uphill to the Franciscan Monastery as the sun casts its magic spell once more.

We stop at a *belvedere* for a spectacular view over Florence, the afternoon sun illuminating the red-tiled city in miniature, its magnificent Duomo but a dot on the horizon.

Inside the monastery, golden light pours into a small, simple courtyard decorated with potted plants; fish dart in a small pond, what once was a well; inside a portico, a fresco of Saint Francis gives his blessing. It's a beautiful, peaceful vibe.

The monastery is full of atmosphere and austerity, the monks' bare cells containing nothing but a writing desk, a cot and an effigy of Christ on the cross. They lived here for most of their adult lives and I ponder such an existence without the comforts of modern life or the caress of a woman.

Ponder over. It's just not me.

Nevertheless, I feel the calm of this place, its devotion and calling clearly tangible.

Slowly making our way out of this tranquil haven in a relaxed state, we get back on two wheels.

Downhill on the back of a *motorino* is a lot faster than uphill. My instincts kick in and I try to sit upright as we camber on each bend, regardless of the laws of physics.

Fortunately, we make another stop, this time to visit Marco's daughter and grandson. Nestled in the trees on the outskirts of Florence, hidden from view, they have the perfect spot. His grandson toddles out with a big smile, arms outstretched. Marco catches him and sweeps him up as sunlight shafts through the trees onto this family moment.

Marco's daughter stands in the doorway holding a tray of glasses and a carafe of water, gesturing us inside to cool down. After introductions, I sit and watch the sweet interchanges of this Italian family. It's touching to see Marco as a father and grandfather.

Back at the flat, my knees are still trembling slightly. Well, more than slightly. No, a lot. Okay, I'm sitting down.

Marco dons an apron and prepares dinner while I recover. Over steak *Milanese*, we share more thoughts on photography and the unique light of Tuscany—there's nowhere in the world where it casts its spell as it does here.

What I notice more than anything about Marco is his love not just for women, but for life, and as I witnessed earlier, for family. He eradicates any judgments I may have had about Italian middle-aged men and sparks up a firm friendship with me as a fellow traveler and creative soul.

By now the couch is calling my name and I have to make friends with it as soon as possible.

A Return to Happeness

After the compulsory *caffè*, I pull out of Marco's. He has a new guest arriving, a young woman. With a manly hug— all the better with someone my own size—we agree to meet up next time I'm in town.

Dropping my bags off at the station, I feel a familiar twang of panic. I don't have a host booked for tonight or tomorrow or for two days after that, but I resolve to not let it get to me. Keep trusting. Something will turn up, remember?

Weaving my way through the tourists, I make my way down the same streets when I first arrived but that profound sense of returning is still just a memory. I'm walking in my usual direction but I'm not really here.

The smell of leather fills the air as I make my way through the busy San Lorenzo market, aisle upon aisle of bags, wallets, belts, jackets, all so much cheaper than the fashion stores. Traders try to Taking the Jump my eye, some calling out to me, but I smile and move on.

Sitting on the steps of San Lorenzo, the panic returns.

Being spontaneous has its advantages, which is part of the appeal of Couchsurfing—meeting new people in new countries with new languages and customs, sharing their homes, going on unforeseen adventures, participating in cultural exchange. Going with the flow. Opening up.

That's the theory, at least.

Right now, I've had enough excitement for a while. I need something stable. I have a headache again and I'm unable to focus clearly. My self-esteem is low and I'm alone again, the lonely drifter with nowhere to go.

Poor me.

Having some degree of self-awareness, I know what this is about. Part of me wants to give up, the part that doesn't care anymore about life, about projects and destiny and making it in the world. The part that wants to die, the deep visceral connection with my mother that wants to join her.

God, that sounds heavy.

As I sit watching the life around me it starts to spatter, the heavens gently anointing me in my melancholy.

Some pretty English girls sit on the steps in front of me, chatting away, laughing at the rain, free twenty-somethings on holiday in Italy. It's a delightful distraction from my inner turmoil and provides a glimpse of the possibility of actually being happy.

In that moment of possibility, my phone vibrates against my leg. Marco's name is on the screen.

"Ciao, Marco."

"Ciao, Navyo. My guest just canceled. Do you have somewhere tonight? You can always come back here if you want."

Accepting his offer, I begin to feel a return to happiness and realize that I can, once more, trust in a power greater than myself. The power that created the situation for his guest to cancel, that knew I needed a place. The power behind the curtains of everyday life.

Slowing
Down

The following morning, I wake up early on Marco's couch refreshed and alive. I don't have to worry about travel and accommodation. I don't have to worry about anything. It will all work out. It always does.

Having just experienced it yesterday, the thought I'm just consoling myself becomes redundant immediately.

Sharing coffee made in his *moka*—I have not been in an Italian home that doesn't have one—Marco lets me leave my bag at his house while I explore more of Florence. He's not only cool, he's kind.

In the shade of tall trees, I walk the footpath along the Mugnone, a small tributary of the Arno, to Piazza della Libertà.

Porticos line the busy streets surrounding the piazza, effectively a park containing a grand triumphal arch and the medieval north gate of the city, Porta San Gallo. In the central pond, a statue of a young woman fights off the advances of a young man.

Taking a closer look, I recognize them as a modern rendition of Daphne and Apollo, when the Gods turned Daphne into a tree to escape Apollo's love-sick desire. Tough luck, Apollo.

Dodging traffic, I board the bus to Piazza San Marco where there's supposed to be free wi-fi. Except there's nothing here but a tiny park with a statue of another ruling-class hero on a horse and busy bus stops unconducive to anything but going somewhere else.

Eventually, I see a sign on the door of the OK Caffè— Firenze Free WiFi. At last.

I sit down and order a fresh-squeezed orange juice and a *panino*. But my enthusiasm for wi-fi quickly wanes as I have to provide my name, nationality, address, date of birth, shoe size and which side I dress, complete with SMS verification, before I can get online.

Each step involves tapping a tiny submit button, not the easiest on my iPhone, which frequently takes me back to the previous screen where I have to enter the information again. By this time my enthusiasm has completely disappeared.

Getting on public internet is a pain in much of Europe. It's still frequently underdeveloped and there are different rules on how it's handled, mostly due to the 'prevention of fraud and terrorism'. Right. Unlike the fast and free, instant-on California.

Finally connected, I make more concerted attempts to find Couchsurfing hosts and realize this is just not going to happen in this town. I am also aware that if it's not happening, it's not meant to happen.

It's at this point I decide to compromise. Shifting to Airbnb, I find three fairly quickly and get a go from Angela, south of the river. Perfect. €35 a night. Booked.

Even though this is against my whole idea of Couchsurfing across Europe, my need for a few nights stability has outweighed my adventurous intentions.

The sense of failure creeps in. What about spontaneous advantages? What about the power behind the curtains? What about trusting in something greater?

Right now, that's all a matter of perspective. The Universe is still working, I'm still acting on what shows up, it's just a change of form. No need to get hung up about it. Accept the fact the I've taken care of myself and I'm going to stay with another local. I'm just paying for it, that's all.

My compromise justified, I finish lunch, pay the bill and take a walk.

I can feel myself slowing down—way down. I'm relaxing with every step, taking in the details I pass by, more open, more available: the sounds of a conversation, the aroma from a cafe, the warmth of the sun.

I make more eye contact with passers by. Most ignore me, but I get the occasional smile, though only from women. It's sad that eye contact with other men has such stigma and double meaning. Tourists are way too involved to notice me, so I deduce these women are Florentine, or at least Italian, each of their smiles an acknowledgment, an affirmation, a connection, however brief.

This is such a change from the stress of not knowing where I'm going to be.

Next time, maybe I can handle it a little differently. Maybe I can slow down, shift perspective and not get so twisted up. Embrace the adventure, trust what's happening, even if I have to pay for it. That whatever it is, by virtue of its existence, is necessary.

The Duomo looms high above the rooftops, its red-brick dome a visual magnet, dwarfing the narrow streets, making them narrower still.

Past an endless row of parked scooters I find a cow. The effigy of this milk-producing bovine can mean only one thing: gelato. But this place is too packed and I'm in no mood to wait when there are so many in Florence, the home of gelato—or so I've been led to believe.

Further down is the less-crowded but highly-rated Mordilatte. Handmade and creamy, this has to be the best I've had so far. Maybe it's because I'm in Florence. Whatever, my taste buds are happy and that happiness is filtering into the rest of my overtired brain.

Back on the steps of San Lorenzo, I watch people come and go. It's such a different experience than yesterday. I feel so dropped in, so in the moment. No concern for the future, just being here.

The sense of giving up I felt earlier has become giving

up the need to be in control. The sense of wanting to die has become dying into the moment.

I slowly make my way to the station for the bus back to Marco's, picking up a bottle of wine for him on the way.

Multilingual Mamma

After promising Marco to catch up next time I'm in town, I roll the Beast out of his apartment and make my way down to the bus stop. Magical Tuscan light illuminates the drama in the skies once more as a full moon rises behind heavy cumulus.

Then comes the 23 Experience.

The bus takes me north, not south, and now I'm back at Piazza San Marco. Frustrated and angry, I haul my bag on another bus going the other direction.

"*Stop, per favore!*" I yell to the driver two minutes later. It's still the wrong bus.

Back over the street, I get on another bus going the original direction. I really don't have a clue where I'm going right now, but at least I'm going somewhere.

The bus takes me in a huge loop around the river, west along the north bank, east along the south bank and finally to my destination, Piazza Gavinana. It's taken me about forty minutes to get here the long way and I'm grumbling about goddamn Italians and their stupid buses.

But Italy is a law unto itself and you've got to take the ride, otherwise you'll spend the entire day frustrated and angry. Things don't work, people are late, nothing is what it seems and the tiniest details can ruin a plan. If you can just let go and relax into the chaos, you'll find *la dolce vita.*

I finally get to the flat and Angela buzzes me up.

Angela is a petite language teacher, fluent in four of them, and she's rented me her bedroom for three nights. Airbnb is a sweet deal for someone wanting to make some extra cash, much needed given the Italian economy. There are those that abuse the concept and there are issues about driving rents up, but when it works it's a win-win.

And it's all the nicer to be in a woman's bedroom. Clean, aesthetic, beautiful.

After showing me around, we sit at the kitchen table and she is shocked to find I have a granddaughter. That compliment makes my day and I retire a happy man, crawling into her bed for a long restful sleep.

The shower is too small for me to stand under. That's understandable as Angela is five-foot-nothing. But hey, I can make it work. Contorting my body into an obscure yoga pose for this very purpose, I manage to soap and rinse myself without breaking the doors of this micro-cubicle.

Clambering carefully out, I unfurl myself with a long

exhale and do my best to dry my wet body with a too-small towel.

Freshened up, I head out for *colazione*—breakfast.

It's raining, but after not too long a walk, I find a spot. Inside Caffè Giannotti, I receive a *buongiorno* and a smile, a welcome touch in tourist-weary Florence.

Sipping *caffè*, my thoughts drift deeper as I watch hypnotic rivulets crawl down the window. It's the perfect time to write about my mother's memorial to share with the rest of my family.

I pull out my laptop and begin to type.

My mother's grandfather, Alfred, whom the family endearingly called Gagga, was born on the Danish island of Aero and emigrated to Scotland in his thirties. My mother always had a strong relationship with him, growing up in Edinburgh. He was a father-figure as her own father died tragically young of tuberculosis.

Her mother, Christiane, spoke Danish with him and they celebrated Christmas Danish style every year on the evening of the 24th with all the red-and-white trimmings.

When she was a teenager, Gagga flew her and her twin sister, Helen, to Copenhagen to introduce them to the Danish family. It was a time she recalled fondly her whole life.

But her lifelong dream of living in Denmark was not to be. She met my father during the Second World War, after which they settled down in England.

In 1959, when I was three, she took me by ferry to

Denmark. Although I was a little too young to remember, it was an important marker in both our lives.

Various members of the Danish family came to visit during the course of her life and the connections remained.

Taking her ashes to Denmark was thus important in many ways, her memorial a highlight to the tumultuous inner journey I've been on since January.

It gave me not just a deeper appreciation of her, but a greater sense of context for my own life. It put me in touch with my inner Dane and gave me direct connection to my ancestor Hans and his bravery as one of the first polar explorers.

I need that courage more than ever.

Being there seems another world to me now. Denmark and Italy are so opposite in so many ways, not just the climate, the culture and the language, but the cold, in-control north versus the loose, hot-blooded Mediterranean south.

While I write, I'm captivated by a song on the radio of a live rock concert filled with Italian passion. I can't get its chorus of *Vivere!* out of my head—or my heart. I don't want to. It brings tears to my eyes.

I ask the girl at the counter, who speaks a little English, who it is. Vasco Rossi, she tells me, a national favorite and a bit of a philosopher.

After a final bout of writing and a second cup of coffee, I get up and pay.

Outside, the rain has stopped, leaving the streets in that soft, relaxing negative-ion state. I take long, slow regenerating breaths as I walk.

At the end of the leafy main street is a giant supermarket, a hypermarket no less. Its cavernous interior is full of people in the way. An assistant pushing a cart filled with produce bumps into me without so much as a *scusi* and starts stocking the shelves.

Italians are a physical people. They're used to body contact, whether it's a shove out the way or an embrace, or a kiss on both cheeks. 'Touch me' is the body language, the signal given out by the look, the pose, the physique, the fashion.

Pushing an old lady aside, I manage to find what I need and head back for lunch and the afternoon's siesta.

Sleeping off a little too much *caffè*, I awake to the sound of raised voices upstairs. A man and woman take turns to voice their opinions at greater and greater volume and accelerating diction. A door slams while the woman continues her volatile monologue, turning into sobs of aloneness.

At this moment, the only thing that appears to make sense in my addled brain is gelato.

Getting some more fresh damp air on the wet sidewalks, I find a small *gelateria* close to Giannotti's and satisfy my craving with a creamy *vaniglia e cioccolato*. Should I get one for the woman upstairs, I wonder?

On my return, all is quiet and Angela, back from work, offers to make dinner.

Over delicious homemade pizza, I learn more about my host. She's a live wire, funny and typically Italian in that expressive, sweetly melodic way.

I mention the neighbors and she rolls her eyes. She tells me about her ex-boyfriend and the fights that used to happen and I begin to understand: pushing, shoving, yelling, sobbing—it's all normal. It's Italian foreplay.

I'm so glad to get out of the story of my mother's death, if just for a while.

Then it dawns on me again—I can enjoy life as well as mourn the loss of my mother. They are not mutually exclusive.

Angela speaks Italian with me to make me practice, interjecting my stumbling attempts like a kind teacher. I could spend a lot more time with her. It's helping me on many levels, not just the language barrier.

San Miniato, Sex and Sin

Angela is a busy woman. Today, she's taking her class to the Uffizi. Heels click on tile as she comes in to say goodbye.

"Please feel welcome. I hope we meet again," she offers with that big smile. "You can leave anytime, just put the keys on the table." And with a *buona giornata,* she walks out the front door.

That level of trust means so much to me as a traveler and as a human being. It's so contrary to the common mindset of fear and protection against strangers, one reinforced in the media and movies over and over. It puts my faith back in humanity.

Over breakfast, I keep getting the hunch to visit San Miniato al Monte, perched high atop a hill overlooking Florence. It's better at sundown, so Marco told me, but I have to go now. According to the map, there's a footpath from the main road that leads all the way there.

It's a beautiful sunny morning with a light breeze, a welcome change from yesterday. Walking up the busy and wide *viale*, I find the entrance to the footpath. Ivy-draped walls and tall trees provide shade as the breeze disappears on my way uphill.

But the quiet tranquility of the path is broken as I come out at the main road again that's looped around. As I wait to cross, I notice a lot of people further down. Walking past empty tour buses to find out, I arrive in the sprawling Piazzale Michelangelo.

A weathered bronze copy of David, green with verdigris, stands resolute in his nudity surrounded by four reclining nudes, each representing a different time of day. More expressions of the human body. But it's the view from the balcony that is truly breathtaking: Florence in all her terracotta glory.

I blend into the tourists for a while and snap accordingly, enjoying the babble of languages. A Chinese couple in full wedding outfits pose for a photo shoot on the balcony below, their candy-pink limousine wrapped in a white bow ruining the elegance of the scene like a giant wad of bubblegum. But who am I to judge.

Close up, David is huge, commanding the view, protecting the city with his naked friends. Street vendors display underwear with photoprints of David's well-hung appendage in the appropriate position. Not only that, there's a whole selection of male genitalia to choose from.

Why on earth would anyone want to wear these?

Whatever it is, it's my cue to leave.

Back on the busy road, I return to the footpath. Winding my way up, it's getting hotter in the morning sun as road noise recedes into the steady rhythm of cicadas. Soon I'm at the top with a hazy panoramic view over Tuscany and the Apennines.

A bell tolls just as I reach the entrance to a cypress grove. What a different vibe than the city streets below, so calm in the shade of these tall trees. I instantly connect with the nature all around me, the throb of cicadas even louder in the heat.

Tucked way up here hidden from view stands a war memorial, a soldier thrusting forward, rifle in hand. In a peace-loving gesture, someone has put flowers in the barrel of his gun.

The path through the cypress grove curves around the monastery of San Miniato, dropping me off at the bottom of the steps leading up to the church. Leaning against the balustrade of the wide stone balcony, I gaze out over the scene before me, Palazzo Vecchio and the Duomo visible through the trees, villas nestled in their gardens below.

Climbing the steps, I turn around to be greeted by yet more magnificent views over Florence and the hills beyond. What a truly awe-inspiring city this is. No wonder it's the home of the Renaissance.

At either side of the steps is a cemetery. Through a low gate, I wander around these temples of the dead, their bronze effigies frozen for eternity—a young barefoot girl on her knees prays over a grave, her hands high in the air; the Madonna opens her cloak, children at her feet reaching up to her. Pity none of them can enjoy the view.

Inside the cavernous basilica, my eyes adjust to the sudden change in light. The sound of heavy flapping cloth approaches behind me as two monks in white cassocks stride past. At the time this was built, apart from bells, birds, footsteps and voices this was the only sound you'd hear.

Giant frescos cover a side wall, partly in shadow; stone pillars and patterned marble lift the eyes up to the timber-framed roof; at the far end, a giant curved mosaic depicts Christ giving his blessing. Up a flight of stone steps, I discover more frescos, more light.

Back down behind the steps is the crypt. While that may sound creepy, it's nothing of the sort. Columns supporting the open arches of the ceiling give an airy feel to this cool sacred space; windows either side shed sunlight onto the floor of flat tombstones, worn smooth; behind an iron grate is its centerpiece, the tomb of San Miniato. Standing in the silence, I imagine the plaintive calls of Gregorian chant.

Outside the church through an archway, I come across an elderly nun, also in white. She smells about four hundred years old and has difficulty talking without many teeth. She's stooped a little with well-worn brown shoes. Nothing about her is attractive, yet she has sacrificed her life to be in service to the church. One must respect such things even if it seems a waste of a life.

I mingle with the tourists in the pebbled piazza in front of the church and find a place to sit. In colorful contrast to the ancient woman whose sexuality has been shamed into extinction, there are quite a few young women up here in big sunglasses, hats and summer clothes, fawning at being in Italy. Such delights are many here and I'm not one to avoid them. There's no shame in that.

Italy is such a place of contrast. Some of the most beautiful women—and men—in the world, the best food in the world, the art, the fashion, the cars, the genital-print underwear—everything about it is sensual and sexual, a passionate, conjugal opera. And yet amidst this sensuality is the Catholic church and its *mea culpa*. Being born is a sin, a sin that comes from the sinful act of sex itself. Maybe this denigration of the body, this shaming and repression of our natural instincts, has created its opposite —the worship of the human form seen in art down the centuries and in modern Italian life.

Italy's physical culture is not a place to hide. Everything is on display and encouraged. It can be quite perplexing to experience such a mixed message.

What happens on a date in this country? I'm so sorry, but I want to take you home and make love to you. Will you forgive me?

Talk about confusing.

Back at the river, a large poster grabs my attention—Niccolò Fabi and his band are performing The Beatles' White Album in its entirety at the amphitheater in Fiesole on that warm summer night in June.

Dancing
Twins

Back in Angela's apartment, it's time to go out again before the row begins upstairs. I look for a *tabacchi*, the tiny shops that sell tobacco, cigarettes, candy, envelopes, stamps and almost anything useful including bus tickets, which is what I'm after. But this is Sunday and they are all closed.

A *pasticceria* is open. I ask the young girl in a blue uniform if she speaks English to no avail. I try some Italian on her but that doesn't work either. Best try my luck elsewhere.

Walking past a grubby condom machine, of which there are a bewildering amount considering contraception is also a sin in Italy, I see it's attached to the front of a *farmacia,* which is open. Maybe they can help me.

Two women and the chemist, all in white lab coats, attend to a pair of identical twin customers, men loudly gesticulating, swaying about the shop as if in some kind of trance. Is this a traditional Italian custom? A dance, maybe? Will they break into the *tarantella* and start rolling around the floor? Or jump on the counter for a routine?

I assume it must be just another Italian conversation and patiently wait for them to finish.

"*Dov'è…um…un biglietto per l'autobus, per favore?*", I ask hesitantly to one of the women, pointing to some coins in my hand.

The woman looks at me, then turns away to continue her conversation with the chemist.

I stand waiting patiently for an answer. Maybe I should start swaying or shouting. Finally she turns to me, informing me in brusk Italian that I must buy the tickets from inside the bus and walks away.

Admittedly, I could have figured this out for myself, but then I'd never have seen the dancing twins.

There's an uneasy relationship with foreigners, especially outside the tourist areas. We're tolerated only because we provide income and even then that tolerance wears thin.

My notion of it being easy to communicate without knowing the language starts to wane.

I return to the apartment and pack, expecting more loud foreplay upstairs. But all is quiet, meaning they are either out, dead, asleep or finished.

Leaving Angela's is somewhat remorseful. I've so enjoyed her company and her apartment, micro-shower and all, and have to pull myself away.

Fortunately, Judith has agreed to put me up for my last night in Florence.

It's a struggle with my bags to get on the bus, but I manage to tender the fare and validate my ticket in the small yellow box as we pull away. It's only a few blocks before I have to get out and change to another bus. As I wait at the stop, the low sun casts its famous light through the trees onto a young couple kissing on a bench.

Ah, Italia.

Weapons of Mass Transportation

Trundling the Beast along the small sidewalk of the small Oltrarno street, I arrive at Judith's just as she walks up to her house. Perfect timing.

We connect over *antipasto*, a Turkish dish from one of her favorite cities, Istanbul—small *crostini* dipped in smoked *melanzane* soaked in lemon and mushed with olive oil. It's delicious.

Like me, Judith is a proud grandparent and full of experience, wisdom and points of view that can only come with maturity and the cultural exposure of world travel. Plus, she's feisty and that's always welcome.

An ardent supporter of the local community and actively engaged in its political struggles, she's a participant not a bystander.

One issue is lethal buses.

At one time, those garish behemoths, the double-decker open-top tour buses even tried to navigate the small streets of the neighborhood.

Now, a regular bus service has been diverted into Oltrarno and it's causing major problems. People are getting hurt. The bus can just about fit, making it a tight squeeze with tall pedestrians like me, who almost got decapitated had I not ducked to avoid the side mirror of the oncoming monster.

Bus drivers in Italy also drive fast. These things hurtle through Oltrarno like they are either making lap time or the driver has an urgent need for a toilet. Whichever the case, they are weapons on four wheels.

So Judith takes to the streets with other concerned locals and demonstrates, a common form of public dissent in demonstrative Italy.

Waking up in the literary confines of her study, I contemplate my tentative future once more and come to a heartening conclusion—even though I may get down and blue and sometimes a nasty shade of brown, I'm always at choice. I don't have to sink to the bottom. I can trust the Universe to guide me, to provide for me. I can have faith.

Confidence. *Con fede*. With faith.

The smell of hot coffee pulls me into the kitchen where Judith has brewed up her *moka* and served us each in a small fine-enameled cup and saucer accompanied by a fresh *brioche*. Sitting at the marble tabletop, I feel the cool of the morning through the open glass-paneled doors of the terrace overlooking the communal garden.

Judith bemoans a story of government corruption she's been reading in the morning's edition of La Repubblica—as if that's ever news in Italy. Regardless, she keeps her finger on the pulse of what's going on.

She's also full of recommendations what I should see during my last day in Florence. Orsanmichele is one, which becomes the purpose of my morning.

A Gory
Lot

Another framed painting of the Madonna and child behind glass adorns a street corner blessing the neighborhood, a reminder that the divine mother is always present.

It's also another powerful moment of realization that even though my own mother is dead, the divine mother is not. Depictions of maternal energy in its highest form surround me in Italy. And when I look around, mothers and mothers-to-be are everywhere.

A market stall full of fresh ripe produce bursts with color in front of me.

With all this abundance of life, death seems so far away, yet without death there would be no life. This simple fact puts much in perspective: I can let my mother rest in peace. I don't have to hold onto the childhood longing for her return or even the fatal wish to join her. I can allow life and nourishment in other forms. I can allow my own life.

I can live without her.

That seemingly obvious adult notion bounces around my brain trying to find somewhere to land. For the grieving child within me, it's a foreign almost unwanted concept, yet I know I have to let it in.

I begin to feel an expansion inside, a stretching. The pain of loss is creating more space, more capacity for experience, for life.

The sense of adventure starts to have deeper meaning. I can bring light into the darkness. It's giving me a willingness, even a desire, to venture into the unknown.

My pilgrimage has become real.

Weaving my way through the maze of Florentine streets, I find the church and museum of Orsanmichele—Orto di San Michele, the Garden of St Michael.

The square building takes up a whole city block and looks nothing like a church as it used to be a grain market. Statues of saints stand in niches on every side. Inside, it's still not much like a church, except for some stained glass and an altar of the Madonna and child inside a huge decorative marble structure, Orcagna's *Tabernacolo*. But it's the ceiling that grabs my attention, its arches and pillars covered in painted designs and frescos.

While that may be worthy of my entire visit, I'm going up to the *primo piano*, the first floor—more confusingly to Americans, the second floor—which contains the museum, only open on a Monday which happens to be today.

Over in the far corner, some tourists enter a small stone archway. That must be it.

Climbing the tight stone spiral staircase, I come out into the museum. Chairs and wooden music stands occupy the central space around two stone pillars, ready for a concert. Large condenser microphones are set up at strategic points indicating it's going to be a broadcast, a recording or both.

Surrounding the performance area are the statues of the museum, Donatello's stoic figures fully clothed.

A more modern spiral stair takes me up to the similarly confusing *secondo piano*.

Entering this large but empty light-filled space that I have almost entirely to myself, I understand Judith's recommendation. Tall windows overlook the terracotta rooftops and there, right in front of me, is the red-brick dome of the Duomo. I let out an audible 'Wow!', turning the heads of a young couple, smiling. This sight alone is worthy of coming here. And it's free.

Wandering through tall arches, each face of the building opens up to another rooftop view of Florence. The campanile of the Badia Fiorentina points to the heavens; through another window, the crenellated parapets of Palazzo Vecchio surround its tower, rising up into another signature image of the Florentine skyline.

I could gaze out of these windows all day.

A sign directs me onto a walkway over the rooftops themselves, providing yet more stunning views, to a descending staircase in the neighboring building and out onto the streets below.

Even though Brunelleschi's red-brick dome is the visual center of Florence, there isn't a clearly defined center once you're at street level, not even Piazza della Repubblica, the original city center—partly because you can't always see the dome in the narrow streets.

The Uffizi, the Bargello, Ponte Vecchio, the Arno, Boboli Gardens, Palazzo Pitti, they all have their own gravitational pull. Now, that gravitational pull is taking me to Piazza della Signoria.

Dominated by the austere Palazzo Vecchio, City Hall, the piazza is filled with more sculptural storytelling.

The Fountain of Neptune is a strange, almost comical affair. A bulky marble Neptune stands in the center surrounded by reclining bronze river gods, laughing satyrs and seahorses. The satyrs, positively alien, lend an absurdity to the scene in stark contrast to the rest of the piazza.

The fountain has been restored countless times due to vandalism, Judith told me. Why would anyone want to destroy such a thing? Is it really that bad?

On one side of the entrance to Palazzo Vecchio stands Michelangelo's David, the feminine grace of his masculine form powerful and spellbinding. Even though it's a marble copy, it's in the location it was intended. He's protecting City Hall, and by association, Florence itself.

The other side of the entrance is the *brutto,* unfeminine Hercules Defeating Cacus. Musclebound and meaty, Hercules stands over Cacus holding his hair in one hand and a large black club in the other.

As if by token gesture, a small figure of a woman stands to one side, Judith Beheading Holofernes. With a raised sword, she is about to commit the act but there's no blood, no resolution. Her victory is implied.

Judith stands for the weak and downtrodden, here at least a symbol for feminine power. Having felt weak and downtrodden lately, I take this as an omen. Judith, my host, has been supportive without the use of a sword, although I'm sure she has one tucked away somewhere.

Walking over to the tall arches of the Loggia dei Lanzi is a much different story, one I can't help but recall from my first encounter last year.

The gory tales from the past still stand, frozen in time. The goriest of these must be Perseus Slaying Medusa by Benvenuto Cellini. Not for the squeamish, blood and gore gush from the neck of naked Medusa, while more blood and gore drip from her severed head, held aloft by Perseus. However violent, the detail of Cellini's work is astounding.

Underneath, a bronze of his naked mother, Danaë, holding his hand as a small boy stands in a niche of the marble pedestal. Did she know what he would grow up to be?

More misogyny continues with the Rape of the Sabine Women. But to my mind, this swirling muscular *ménage-à-trois,* originally untitled, is more a symbol of feminine freedom than male dominance. It's a spectacular rendition of the human form in motion and nothing about the title which was added later.

Then we're back to clubbing and killing.

Hercules defeating the centaur, Nessus, is more macho male superiority. Then there's The Rape of Polyxena, this time clearly unambiguous—a naked woman being dragged off against her will, another about to be slain, and a man, their would-be rescuer, dead on the ground.

I detect a deep insecurity in the Italian male mind to commission, create and display such dominance and violence towards women. It's not as if this ever went away.

David at least emanates grace after his defeat of another archetype of male dominance, the giant Goliath. Considering the sexual tendency of Michelangelo, maybe this was intentional, given the *machismo* around him.

Inside the courtyard of Palazzo Vecchio, I start to cool down. Every square inch of the inner portico's arched ceiling has been decorated, each column covered in a gold-plaster relief of patterns and motifs; depictions of foreign cities line the walls; the statue of a winged child holding a small dolphin stands atop the central fountain. He's not about to cut its head off or club it to death. It's the antithesis of what's outside.

Taking more respite from the bloody violence of the piazza, I walk towards the river with the slow parade of tourists as they head for Ponte Vecchio, the Old Bridge.

The tour groups clogging the bridge are daunting and

there are already more approaching. It's starting to feel like Venice. I make my way through the multitude, the sound of German and Chinese a harsh contrast to lyrical Italian.

In medieval times, the goldsmiths lining either side of the enclosed bridge used to be butchers until the smell got so rank they were kicked out, or so I read. Along the top of the bridge is a section of the Vasari Corridor. Stretching from Palazzo Pitti across the Arno to the Uffizi, it was built by Giorgio Vasari, architect, artist, writer and impresario for the ruling Medici, so they could move unnoticed.

Released from the crush, I leave the tour groups and cut down towards Palazzo Pitti.

Across from the *palazzo* is a small shop selling artisan teas and chocolate.

As I close the door behind me, the old woman behind the counter calls to the back. A beautiful woman in her forties appears, presumably her daughter, as is the business tradition in Italy, and her mother presents her with a knowing smile and a nod. We're back at medieval court and I am some foreign suitor. Should I bow and kiss her hand? It's a completely unexpected, theatrical moment.

She proudly shows me her chest full of exotic teas and asks if I want to smell them. The bouquets bombard my senses in an aromatic hallucination and I can't quite believe what's happening.

Where am I? When am I? Is this another *commedia dell'arte?*

I should have brought my lute.

I choose a blend of rose and darjeeling for Judith, thank the woman and her mother and leave the shop unbetrothed.

Dinner to Die For

Tonight, Judith has invited me to dinner at the best trattoria in Florence, she assures me. People are lining up to get in and we get an early table as she is a frequent patron.

The menu is meat-heavy, as favored by the Florentines. She recommends not the two-inch-thick heart-stopping steak, but the *bollito misto,* a traditional dish that is to die for, she assures me. Okay, I'll buy that. You live here, you know best.

After not too long a wait and a lively discussion about Florentine politics, beheadings and misogyny, dinner is served.

What arrives on my plate looks like body parts from the floor of an abattoir. I do my best, but honestly, this is disgusting. Of course, I don't say that. I'm trying to be polite.

What is this, exactly? I'm not quite sure. It looks like a large animal penis with some cartilage to maintain its erection. It's white with some brown parts. The other meat on my plate is also white and brownish and it's all been boiled to death. Maybe the abattoir is next door. Maybe the animals are being boiled alive in a massive pot. Something nasty is going on in the kitchen, I can sense it.

Wait, there's something green on my plate. That's encouraging. I try a bite and it's as bitter as bitter can be, and then some. No, I can't eat this. Or that. Or the other thing.

Maybe it's the dish. There are probably other things on the menu that are perfectly edible but it's all too late now. The line has gotten longer and Judith is almost finished. She comments on my pallor, my expression and my lack of appetite and I have to admit my reluctance to indulge in such carnage.

This is not dinner, it's a medical experiment.

Even though our tastes divert on the table, Judith and I maintain a mutual passion for life and travel. I tell her I'll be in Palermo, Sicily, in three weeks time and by coincidence, she's going to be there visiting friends.

We arrange a date to meet for lunch.

I look forward to trying something different. Something vegetarian.

Woman
on Top

After a final breakfast with Judith in the cool of her kitchen, I pack and get ready to leave. She has been a most genial host, *au courant*, spirited and culinarily diverse.

Avoiding the cost of a taxi, I make the manly, slightly Herculean choice of dragging the Beast, along with my heavy shoulder bag, all the way to the station.

Alternating between the roads and the small sidewalks involves more bumpy cobblestones, loose flagstones and the occasional pothole, not to mention other people. It's a drag in more ways than one.

Thirty minutes later, I arrive at the *deposito bagagli* on platform sixteen and lighten my load. Freed of bags, I take my last wander in Florence for a while.

I'm getting used to all these people by now. I've learned to flow, to anticipate, to sidestep and on occasion to barge. Ideally, take a backstreet and avoid people altogether.

Past rows of the inevitable designer shops in mercantile Florence, past Palazzo Strozzi, I walk through a monumental arch and arrive in Piazza della Repubblica, the old market square. Tourists and locals alike populate the open space. It's easy to spot the difference—tourists stop and stare; the locals are going somewhere.

In the middle of the piazza, the statue of a woman holding an overflowing cornucopia stands atop a column, representing a good harvest and bringing prosperity to the city. For such a prosperous place and the home of the Medici bankers, I'm not sure she's necessary.

Like the locals, I'm just passing through. I've taken up one of Judith's other recommendations—I'm on my way to see more statues of naked people.

The Bargello holds the largest collection of Renaissance statues in Italy, not that I'm not going to see them all. Even though I walked out of the Strozzi grumbling about statues in galleries, I pay the entrance fee and go in.

Porticos surround a courtyard with a central well, around which a stage is built for concerts. It's the perfect setting and I can just imagine a chamber orchestra playing Vivaldi on a warm evening. Only later will I find out this historic setting was the location for executions, mostly beheadings with a few hangings.

A group of naked figures forming a fountain overlook the stage from the back wall. A woman, the only figure fully clothed, presides on top of a slender arch with two peacocks either side; inside the arch, a man reclines on one side while on the other, a woman rests on a large overturned urn between her legs where water would gush forth; in the center, a woman stands holding her breasts where more water would burst out, a cheeky grin on her face.

These figures of the Sala Grande Fountain each represent various gods and goddesses in a playful, erotic celebration of water, if only it were turned on.

On the second floor, or the first depending where you're from, in a huge room with a high vaulted ceiling, a crowd gathers around a small, rather effeminate male nude cast in dark bronze, standing with one foot on a very large severed head.

This is Donatello's David, very different from Michelangelo's larger-than-life poetic vision of the male body.

I eavesdrop on an English-speaking docent, who informs her group that, "in 1430, this was the first sculpted male nude since Roman times." That took a while.

The architectural scale surrounding it makes this David even more diminutive and adds to the grandeur of the Bargello. Ignoring the sign telling me not to, I take a photo incurring a maternal reprimand from one of the staff as she runs towards me wagging her finger. It's not as if she confiscates my iPhone or asks me to leave. I've just given her the pleasure of doing her job.

Inside a portico sits yet another beautiful naked woman—I've lost count by now—representing the profession of architecture. Sculpted by Giambologna, his Naked Allegory is supposedly of divine proportion. She's mesmerizing. Not only that, she's got natural curves and weight to her, a fleshy sexual power unlike the modern-day stick figures that the media and fashion industry dictate.

More nudes populate the upper gallery, all worthy of the entrance fee partly due to the Bargello being such an atmospheric, historical space. It's as if they were meant to be here. Nothing like the Strozzi.

Situated in a strategic position on the lower floor is a message in marble. This time the woman is on top, literally. A classically-formed naked woman is overcoming an old man, crouched and submissive between her powerful legs. She represents Florence and the old man Pisa, showing which city has the upper hand—and the rest.

This is what I love about Italians. Even though the subject matter of their depictions may be *risqué* and at times bloody, they have perfected the human form in both art and flesh, transporting us to the heights of desire and beauty. It's definitely worth fighting for.

Back on the street, there's just enough time for *caffè* and I call Marco to see if he wants to join me. Alas, he's busy and wished I'd called earlier. He would have loved to go for lunch together so I could try his favorite *lampredotto*, a popular street food in Florence. It sounds tasty, whatever it is.

I look up *lampredotto* on my phone and find it is a

tripe sandwich made from the cow's fourth stomach, an anatomical feature I did not know. The Daily Telegraph compared it to 'eating your own tongue, excreting it whilst ripping out your own anal sphincter, vomiting over it, then slapping it in a roll.'

I'll have to recommend it to Judith, although it's probably her favorite too.

Picking up my bags at the station, I board the train and sleep all the way to Rome.

ROME

The Eternal City

Making my way through Termini, the bustling central station, I step out into the wide streets, trams, buses, cars, people, noise and life of Rome. Florence seems quaint by comparison. It's been eight months since I was here for that epic bike ride, the Ciemmona, and I'm soaking up every second.

Down Via Cavour on this hot, sunny day, Beast in tow, past the back of Santa Maria Maggiore, past the newsstand on the corner, past the metro station, Elite supermarket, the Borgia steps, memories come flooding back to life.

A block away, I see Alessia at her door with her sweet little dog, Kira. Perfect timing yet again.

After warm hellos, I wrestle my bags into the tiny lift and ride up to her apartment while she and Kira take the stairs.

Through the security gate and the heavy polished-wood front door, I step into that familiar feeling again—the tall ceilings, the smooth tile floor, the kitchen, the fridge covered in notes, magnets and messages, some boxes in the hallway, a book on the table, all the signs of her life.

Connecting over tea, I see again how Alessia is so considerate and caring and genuinely interested. It's still a surprise to have someone listen after the short attention spans I got accustomed to in the States.

She's going to spend most of the time at a friend's, so I've got the place pretty much to myself.

After a change of clothes, I take off for a walk and some context.

Oh, how I love Rome. Every street, every corner holds a view of history, of Italian style and the modern day. Centuries of the passionate chaos of life and art has given rise to the most epic city in the world. There is nothing like it.

As the light begins to fade and streetlamps flicker, I breathe in this awesome place and let it take me, every step a step into the moment.

Down at the Colosseum, I sit on a bench on this warm evening as floodlights illuminate the spectacle while people gaze up in communal wonder. It's hard not to.

Joining them in front of the giant arena, I begin to sense the focal point of where I stand—to my right, the newly restored Arch of Constantine, the Celian and Palatine hills beyond it either side; behind me, Via Sacra, the Sacred Way, leading up to the Arch of Titus and the Forum. I'm at the epicenter of Ancient Rome.

Something stirs within me, some far distant memory, some recognition.

Back in Monti, the oldest district of Rome, I wander its tiny cobbled streets, a village within the city, and re-accustom myself from last year. It's like I never left.

Unlike the tourist areas, it's quiet here. Through the window of a trattoria, people sit eating, faces aglow in candlelight, sipping wine, the chaos of voices filling the air as I pass by its open front.

Cascades of ivy drape the buildings either side of me; more ivy spans a side street forming a canopy; potted plants decorate front doors; flowers and greenery trail from window boxes—the entire place is a magical garden.

Voices become louder as I enter Piazza Madonna, filled with locals sitting around the fountain. I sit among them, the chorus of *italiano* surrounding me as I relax into being here.

Returning to the flat, my senses satiated, I crawl into bed and sleep.

Waking up on my first day here, I spend the morning planning and budgeting. Money is getting low and I use it as a test in trust. More will come exactly when I need it, just like it's always done.

But now it's time to get out of numbers and into Rome.

Walking back up Via Cavour to Termini, I turn left to arrive at the giant roundabout that is Piazza della Repubblica. Flanked by tall, curved porticos on one side, its centerpiece is a joyfully erotic fountain, the Fontana delle Naiadi. A man holds a large fish, gushing water high in the air; around him are four naked nymphs, each in a prone position of pleasure with creatures of the sea. Apparently, this aquatically racy piece was deemed too erotic when it was built in 1901 and was to be moved somewhere less conspicuous, but this being Rome, sensuality prevailed.

Opposite the fountain on the other side of the piazza is the Basilica of Santa Maria of the Angels and Martyrs. Unassuming from the outside, this magnificent place is one of my favorite churches in Rome. The vast structure used to be the baths of Emperor Diocletian until a certain Michelangelo Buonarroti transformed it into a sacred space. It was his last work completed when he was eighty-five years old.

Even though much of the decoration, added later during the Baroque era, is *trompe l'œil* and not three-dimensional stucco or marble, the power of the space is intact. It's as if the emptiness itself is encouraging, holding the divine.

High up in a corner, a small hole allows a single beam of sunlight onto the floor. Every day at noon, the beam crosses a long bronze strip at a different place according to the change of seasons, marked on either side with star coordinates, the names of constellations and images of the zodiac.

This arcane device called the Clementine Gnomon after its commissioner, Pope Clementine XI, was used to correctly determine Easter, different every year.

At the end of the strip closest to the wall are a series of concentric ellipses, also in bronze, to track the path of the pole star. These guys were into some serious astronomy.

As astronomical measurement can be traced back to the Arabs, not only do we have pagan astrology but Muslim astronomy in a Catholic church.

Hmm.

Walking back across the marble floor, worn smooth over the centuries, I have to question the symbolism at my feet. Inlaid in the pink marble is a flower which on closer inspection resembles male and female genitalia on the brink of union. Really? Was this intentional? Or is this natural marbling illustrating a counterpoint to the virgin birth? Is it a desecration? Or am I having a Rorschach moment?

Hard to tell, but impossible to miss.

Outside the basilica, I don my wide-brimmed sun hat in full view of a street vendor.

"Cowboy!" he yells over to me. "Want a tour of Rome?"

"*No, grazie*", I reply with a wave and a hurried gait.

He starts to follow me, shouting more offers as I quicken my stride. He clearly has me in his sights. I turn and face him, my hand outstretched.

"NO!"

Out comes a blast of Italian expletives I don't care to understand far less translate. He walks away, grumbling and gesticulating, eyeing the territory for his next meal. A better approach might increase his chances.

Further down is the church of Santa Maria della Vittoria which holds possibly the most controversial religious artwork not just in Rome, but the whole world.

Inside, the drama of Catholicism comes to life. Every surface of the church is decorated in Baroque splendor. Sculpted white angels and cherubs, or *putti*, surround the ceiling fresco, the Triumph of the Virgin Mary over Heresy —naked sinners fall into a mass of dragons and books while the Virgin sits on a cloud gazing up to heaven. Best not to read.

But it's the scene at the back that causes a stir.

The Ecstasy of Saint Teresa is one of the most striking depictions of divine possession—or in this case, penetration—ever created. This religious erotica, a strange and frequent paradox in Rome, is another of the Baroque master Gianlorenzo Bernini, whose work decorates much of the city.

In what appears to be a small stage, Saint Teresa lies prone on her back in a state of physical ecstasy while a smiling angel stands next to her holding his golden arrow in one hand and lifting up her dress with the other. Golden light beams down behind them.

Figures in theatrical boxes either side ogle at her climax.

Is it pornography? Or is it genuine spiritual rapture?

With the angel lifting up Teresa's dress, her prostrate position, closed eyes and open mouth, it seems this was not an abstract experience.

In a more progressive view, the line between sex and spirituality is blurred, the act of procreation by its very nature holy. Maybe Bernini had this secretly in mind. It's astonishing he got away with it and makes the ceiling fresco even more confusing.

Across the street from the church, Moses points his finger accusingly as lions either side spout water from their lips. Giggling Japanese girls pose for a photograph, adding levity to the biblical commandment.

What a conundrum is Rome, the mix of the sacred and profane becoming more evident at every turn. It seems the city itself is built of divine union. Being here fills both the senses and the spirit in a way that feels whole as well as holy.

Downhill, a giant open clamshell stands on a corner of Piazza Barberini. This is the Fontana delle Api, the Fountain of the Bees. Three bees, the symbol of the wealthy Barberini family, sit in the basin of the clamshell, also designed by the ubiquitous Bernini, which makes it a Baroque Bernini Barberini bee basin.

The more palatable Fontana del Tritone, again by Bernini, is the impressive centerpiece of the piazza. The water god Triton, depicted as a muscular merman, blows water high in the air from a conch while perched on yet another open clamshell held by the tailfins of four dolphins. And yes, in the tails of these dolphins are the bees of the Barberini family crest, making it one more Baroque Barberini Bernini.

The elegant porticos of Palazzo Barberini, the home of this powerful bee-loving family, provide shade in the heat of the day. Avoiding the art exhibition inside, I wander through its arches into a beautiful landscaped garden behind the palace, yet another hidden gem inside the city.

I sit awhile amidst the greenery and let myself be here.

Is this really happening? Am I really in Rome?

Stepping out of this sanctuary, I'm back on the streets relaxed and refreshed.

Four fountains, the Quattro Fontane, are built into the walls of a crossroads in their respective directions. Each fountain contains a figure in repose, two of them female holding the neck of a swan in yet more erotic suggestion. Dirty from pollution but still beautiful, they reflect the state of the city. Of course, the *municipio* can clean them up if they want, but decay seems to be favored around here. After all, it's part of the charm of Rome.

Walking these busy streets I feel the life all around me, the buzz, the rhythm of the city beating with a heart so old, so powerful, it seems it will never end. People have come and gone for centuries, mothers have bred generations, yet Rome still stands.

This glimpse of eternity helps redefine my mortal loss —my mother may be gone but I am still here.

Back home, I take a well-earned nap.

Taking my sunset stroll of Rome, a daily occurrence, I join locals and tourists alike on the evening *passeggiata,* the communal walk to relax after the day, to meet friends and to see and be seen, a long-held tradition in Italy.

Via dei Fori Imperiali, the street of the Imperial Forums, is a wide thoroughfare leading from Piazza Venezia to the Colosseum, built by Mussolini in the 1930s. There's little or no traffic except an occasional bus, taxi or police car. It's ideal for a stroll.

While that might be a nice thing, Mussolini demolished treasures of Ancient Rome and the Renaissance to make his statement.

Walking towards Piazza Venezia, I stop and lean over the railings. The crumbling traces of power and empire lie before me, broken columns still standing, steps leading up to what once was.

A ramp leads down into Emperor Trajan's Forum where you can wander through the remains. Behind it stands Trajan's Market, the Roman shopping mall. Small arches perforate the side of the curved building, each for a different merchant, windows into a world long gone.

At the far end is Trajan's Column, a winding frieze of heroic storytelling going all the way up, at one time, to the man himself. On the other side of the road, Julius Ceasar, hand raised, announces his own forum.

Taken as a whole, these atmospheric ruins provide the

stage set for the *passeggiata*. There's been talk of tearing up the road and turning it into a protected archeological site. I'd vote for that.

I check out the timing of Colosseum tours on my iPhone and decide to go and buy a ticket for tomorrow. But I've overlooked one vital piece of information—by the time I arrive, the ticket office has closed.

Momentarily disappointed, I walk up Via Sacra towards the Forum as sunlight streams down through the Arch of Titus. There's no way disappointment can survive this.

On a wall to the left of the closed gates, a small sign inscribed in stone reads Alla Chiesa di S. Bonaventura, indicated by an arrow underneath. Following its directive uphill, the intoxicating scent of jasmine fills the air as sunset over the Forum appears before me.

Long shadows of broken temples, villas and grand arches fall amongst the ruins. A voice over the tannoy ushers out the day's last visitors, tiny figures in the remains.

Further up, the hypnotic rhythm of cicadas surrounds me as golden light glows around the garden gates of San Sebastiano. There's an unmistakable sense of the sacred.

At the top of this tiny winding hill, the scuffed, cracked stucco of San Bonaventura burns a rich red ochre. Breathing deeper, slower now, the power of this place fills me.

Rome, truly the Eternal City.

Another Afternoon
Agenda

Elite, as its name suggests, is the local upscale supermarket. Even though it's pricey, it stocks more of what I'm after as opposed to the mini-markets that abound around here.

Purveying the deli counter, I spy my favorite.

"Un po' mozzarella di bufala per una persona, per favore," I ask the man behind the counter.

Immaculately groomed in a clean white shop coat, he carefully removes the fresh mozzarella from the glass case as if he's holding a baby.

Cutting part of the large white ball, he weighs it, places it in a plastic bag, adds some water, seals it tight, sticks on the label and passes it to me like a midwife.

"È tutto, signore?" he inquires.

"Sì, grazie mille."

I grab some ripe, deep red *pomodori* and fresh *basilico* on my way out, a combination that is a staple in Italy and for good reason.

Back home, I make lunch from this bounty—*insalata caprese*—each portion drizzled with olive oil and some very old balsamic vinegar I found in Alessia's cupboard. The mix of textures and flavors brings not only a smile but a satisfaction only attained in this country. Even if that is to a degree psycholocational, the ingredients are unattainable elsewhere. Exports are never the same as what's locally produced and consumed. By the time anything this fresh is shipped to London or San Francisco, it's lost its manna.

The delights of my digestion prompt visions of all things Italian. I set my sights on Caravaggio, the Tiber and the Vatican, and will accomplish all three this afternoon.

Taking the metro to Flaminio, I walk over busy streets into the vast Piazza del Popolo where the Basilica di Santa Maria sits just inside the giant ceremonial gate. Unlike museums, entrance is free and I've heard the church contains Caravaggios worthy of a visit. But my timing goes awry as the doors are locked until four.

The lack of Caravaggio provides a brief walk—unheard of for a Roman—around the piazza. I could easily stay here the rest of the day sipping *caffè* at Canova's, people-watching, or at least until four o'clock, but I can't hang around.

Crossing the Tiber, I walk along its banks until I come to the heavenly Ponte Sant'Angelo, one of the icons of Rome with angels lining either side of the bridge. It's also more of maestro Bernini decorating the city.

But behind Bernini's beauty lies a dark history.

Across the bridge, Castel Sant'Angelo looms menacingly. Originally a mausoleum for Emperor Hadrian, it was used at various times as a fortress, a papal residence and a prison, with torture and executions a normal occurrence.

Turning my back on this edifice of atrocities, I walk in the direction of another site of questionable repute—the Vatican.

While that admonition may offend, its reputation before the Protestant Reformation included papal orgies, sodomy and incest to name a few. A tad hypocritical or the work of fiction?

The road approaching St. Peter's is an impressive driveway to the home of the Catholic Church. There is no traffic except from a controlled cross street with barriers either side, an armored vehicle and some patrolling *carabinieri*, guns at the ready.

Closer to the piazza, vendors are selling all kinds of Catholic trinkets, photos of the pope, rosaries, miniatures of St Peter's, but unlike Piazzale Michelangelo in Florence, no male genital-print underwear, even with a fig leaf.

The circular expanse of St Peter's Square is packed with pilgrims creating a line around its colonnaded circumference, another Bernini touch, before snaking their way up the steps into the basilica. There's no way I'm going to get in and it's not just because of the line. I don't care how famous it is or how much I should see it or the Sistine

Chapel, it's not a happy place, at least not for me, not now.

I feel a disturbing energy, thick and dark, echoing the screams of tortured heretics down the road. No, thank you. But that hasn't stopped the tourists from flocking.

Back over the river, my mood begins to lighten as I weave my way down colorful busy pedestrian streets. Up a flight of steps, I go inside a church in hope of some artistic redemption.

The frescos adorning the cupola of Sant'Agostino, the colors, the statues, the light, everything in this ornate interior imparts the glory of devotion. Its heavenly explosion of shape and color divests me of any bad vibes I arrived with.

The paradox of the Catholic Church with its dark and bloody history that has given form to some of the most divine artwork ever created is one I struggle to accept. Light and dark, heaven and hell, the spiritual *chiaroscuro* created by these polarities seems more understandable now. Maybe this is the appeal of Caravaggio, the master of shadow and light.

Feeling better, I make my way to another of my favorites haunts, the Pantheon. This is part of the joy of Rome, everything is so close.

There's an art to doing nothing and sitting around a fountain in a piazza in Rome is the place to do it, especially this one, Piazza della Rotonda. The water, the babble of foreign tongues, the warm evening, the gentle melody of a guitar drifting through the air, the whole place is made for doing nothing, something Romans are famous for.

Across the piazza stands its monumental focal point, the Pantheon. The last intact building from Ancient Rome, it's a phenomenal feat of engineering with a free-standing concrete dome, once covered in bronze. This pagan temple of the many Gods, hence Pantheon, is now a consecrated church, but that doesn't stop its original purpose from coming through.

It's been used for state funerals and stage sets, appearing in numerous films much like the rest of Rome.

A long line four and five-abreast gradually moves towards the entrance between the sixteen giant columns of the portico. Undaunted, I join them and slowly make my way inside.

Even though I was here last year, the interior is still a sight to behold. Light pours down from the oculus illuminating the vast circular space. Even with the crowd, it manages to feel empty such is the ingenuity of its design, its height and diameter the same.

The beautiful marble floor is the only thing impossible to fully appreciate with everyone here. Altars recess behind columns around the circumference; statues of saints stand in niches. I can't help wonder what it was like without all the Christian additions. But the eye always roves upward to the oculus, open to the heavens, rain or shine.

Amongst all this devotion, history and sheer size, I have another strange, almost illusory moment—regardless of all the people around me, I feel alone. Not the lost and alone I felt in Florence, but the pure aloneness of being, of being here in this sacred space, this temple. It's as if everyone just disappeared and I'm left with light and emptiness.

Is this what dying feels like?

The chaos of voices suddenly brings me back and I wend my way outside.

Sitting at the base of a column in the portico, I watch the scene—people coming and going, sitting around the fountain, the unmistakable strains of Wish You Were Here from the guitarist in the piazza returning me to present-day life in Rome.

After yet another well-earned nap back at the apartment, I'm out again for the sunset stroll.

This special time of day yields the most amazing light over the Colosseum, billows of cumulus aglow with the setting sun, the sky reflecting the drama below. I sit and watch as the clouds evolve, colors deepen and the light slowly fades over Ancient Rome.

By now it's dark and I'm hungry. Crossing Via Cavour, I head into Monti for something to eat. Wanted is a popular spot and on perusing the menu, I decide to go in.

Even though Italians eat their salad after the main course, I order an *insalata di rucola* first. The waiter is accustomed to this so he doesn't object, but given my preclusion for authenticity, I feel a bit of a tourist.

After a long wait sipping *acqua frizzante,* spinach

tortelloni in a rich cream sauce arrives, preceding the requested salad. He has followed tradition and I'm not going to argue.

The *tortelloni* are delicious and the salad, well, more of a digestive aid than anything. But I got to eat and I'm full and happy. Considering the plight of my less-fortunate fellow homeless travelers, I feel privileged.

Stepping out into the warm night air, I'm ready to chill. It's been a long day doing nothing.

Just around the corner, Piazza Madonna is abuzz with locals again. I find a spot on the steps of the fountain, feeling, if just for a while, that I'm one of them.

Bloodbaths, Virgins and Murder

By the time I get to the Colosseum, it's clear I have the advantage. I'm the first in line to buy a ticket this early morning and proceed through the gates into what was at one time the scene of a daily bloodbath.

I should have brought my hat. The sun is already hot and the wind is playing havoc with my hair, a valid concern for a vainglorious vagabond such as myself.

Up well-trodden steps and out into the public level, this vast elliptical space dwarfs the other people arriving, mere specks amidst the ruins. The scope and scale of this place is mindblowing—until I hear the details of its deadly past.

Earbuds installed, renowned travel guide Rick Steves provides the perfect audio tour as I walk around the monumental arena.

The Colosseum was home to some very bad things.

Violent death was celebrated in all its gory detail. Life was sacrificed without concern but for sport and enjoyment. Christians and animals were slaughtered *en masse*. Men were pitted against each other to the death. Gladiatorial combat went all the way. No one was spared. It was even filled with water for naval reenactments. The Romans were into spectacle.

The design of the Colosseum was cutting-edge. They created this thing to hold up to eighty thousand people. The arena could be emptied in a matter of minutes through a passageway for each seating tier, known appropriately as a *vomitorium*.

A certain few, however, were barred from entering, including ex-gladiators and actors. The irony.

Next time, I have to take the underground tour to experience what it was really like down there, that dank and sorry place where the poor victims were kept, listening to the crowd roar for their death.

Even though magnificent in scale and engineering—its structural concept still employed in modern arenas—the whole place is a chilling reminder, even on this hot, sunny day: we may gape at our past and wonder at its marvels, but the purpose of the Colosseum is not one to indulge in again.

Back home, I opt for something far more civil and take Alessia's dog Kira for a walk around the block. Leash in hand, she makes me feel even more like a local.

Relaxing after a late lunch, I hear Alessia come in the front door and we sit and chat over some mint tea. Not one to espouse opinions and brandish her ego, she asks questions, gently probing for deeper meaning, taking a genuine interest in life and others. Some of those questions don't even have answers, but open up a conversation, a connection. That's a rare and valued quality in my book.

Following my experience at the Colosseum this morning, I go to the Forum to complete my tour of Ancient Rome as my ticket is good for both.

The Roman Forum, or Foro Romano, is just as atmospheric as the Colosseum, maybe more so, but without the blood. Rick Steves educates me once more, guiding the way. It's indispensable to have an audio tour of the Forum, otherwise you're just looking at a crumbled mess of rubble and remains without much of a clue.

Listening to the tour, the Forum becomes vivid and alive, a stage set for the imagination.

The Forum was the center of everyday life in Ancient Rome—markets, meetings, speeches, court hearings, triumphal processions, banquets, prostitution (legal back then); you name it, it went on here.

Three huge arches tower above me. Massive is an understatement. And these were just to support the main arches that went higher still, spanning over to the other side. This is all that's left of the Basilica of Constantine (or the earlier Maxentius, depending on which Emperor you prefer).

Everything was built on a grand scale to make you humbled by the power of Imperial Rome.

These days, the term basilica is used for a large Christian church built on a similar floor plan, but here it was a gargantuan meeting hall put to various uses. At one end was a colossus of Emperor Constantine. Now only bits of him are left—a foot, a pointing hand, his head—put on display in the Capitoline Museum.

Further inside the Forum stand three columns, the remains of a circular temple. This was the Temple of Vesta, goddess of hearth and home. As long as the sacred flame burned inside, Rome would continue. Keeping that flame alive was the job of the Vestal Virgins, six priestesses chosen at the early age of ten with a vow of chastity that lasted thirty years. With routine inspections, any of them found not to be intact were given a loaf of bread—not the sort of punishment I had imagined—and then buried alive.

No cheese or olive oil, then.

Apart from the risk of a slow and suffocating death, the perks of the job were socially upmarket, such as the power to pardon condemned criminals and having your own box at the Colosseum opposite the Emperor.

The Virgins lived next to the temple in the aptly named House of the Vestal Virgins, a long two-story villa in typical Roman style with a central courtyard and fountain surrounded by porticos.

As well as tending the sacred flame, their duties

included carrying sacred water from a sacred spring and cooking sacred food on their own sacred fires. Were there sacred toilets, I wonder?

If they remained virgins for thirty years, they were given a handsome severance package and allowed to marry. I can imagine the honeymoon. Strange, painful, awkward, terribly late yet absolutely necessary.

Unfortunately, many women broke their vows only to suffer their dark, suffocating fate without going hungry. Which proves that sometimes, satisfying basic human needs are more important than consequences.

Tucked away at the back of the Forum under a tin roof behind a low wall is the altar to the murdered Balding Adulterer, more popularly known as Julius Ceasar. The altar marks the site of the Temple of Ceasar as he was declared divine after his death and his sins forgiven. Flowers and handwritten notes still decorate his shrine two thousand years later.

After a full day of bloodbaths, virgins and murder, I come back to the flat and lie down, integrating the stories of the past with the reality of today. Ancient Rome is still alive in the ruins and playing out in modern life.

La
Ciemmona

I've spent the morning organizing travel, booking flights and skipping breakfast. Around noon, Alessia offers me a welcome brunch which we share together. It's a bit of a quiet table and I feel surprisingly awkward, but after some warming up, we finally connect.

I ask Alessia if I can leave my bags here while I go to Naples and Sicily and she obliges. Not only that, she has a bag I can use for carry-on. Perfect.

By now it's three o'clock, time for me to pick up the bicycle I reserved at the local rental shop. Ever since I rode the Ciemmona last year, Rome's answer to San Francisco's Critical Mass bike protest rally against too many cars and too much pollution, I've been waiting to do it again. It was an experience that warm full-moon night I shall always remember. The only difference now is Alessia won't be there. I'll miss her.

Sailing down Via Cavour on my sturdy black 15-speed Ghost, I head for Piazza Madonna to hook up with the Monti crew. There's already some folks waiting, adjusting their bikes. A few more show up and soon enough, we're ready to roll.

Following the pack leader, we ride shotgun up Via del Corso, cutting over to the Spanish Steps, past all the tourists, across Piazza del Popolo and straight up to the Sport Palace to convene with the mass.

This is the Ciemmona's Tenth Anniversary and it's a big deal. The huge parking lot of the Sport Palace is already overflowing with *ciclisti* ready for action.

Giangi rides up and gives me a hug, a big grin underneath his cycling cap, eyes sparkling. It's good to see him again since last year's epic ride. He rolls a cigarette while we catch up a little. He's going to be at Alessia's in a few days and we agree to meet.

It's not too long before whistles begin to blow, music starts to blare and we begin to move. Bit by bit, we file onto the main road to head down the Lungotevere running beside the Tiber back into town. I've lost count of how many we are, but we must be well over a thousand.

We stop at traffic lights and wait for the convoy to catch up. Locals lean out of their windows to watch. Music fills the streets from portable sound systems rigged to bike trailers. Some have wine or beer kegs with long drinking straws for other riders. Some riders are in costume. Some bikes are hybrid art pieces with double frames welded onto each other. It's one big party on wheels.

At this point, we're pretty dense and no traffic can either get through us or stop us. We've taken the streets, albeit temporarily, and it feels a socially empowering act. Riding through an underpass, more whistles blow and airhorns fire. This is loud. Thunder rolls above as if to echo our cacophony.

I'm riding close to the front. Ahead of us is a sight that makes me both scared and worried with a dose of panic. A line of *carabinieri* in soldier's fatigues are linked arm-in-arm across the road.

Almost.

They've left the sidewalks empty.

The mass diverges like the Red Sea, flowing around the *carabinieri*, who start frantically shouting and waving at their lost cause. You can't stop a thousand cyclists with a handful of policemen. They give up and stand back to watch as we all ride by. It's a classic Italian example of *brutta figura* that manages to be both endearing and inept.

There's no rush for backup, no sirens wailing, no guns drawn against this civil disobedience. It's another reminder of how different life is outside America.

By the time we get to the Colosseum, it's been drizzling for half an hour and there are a lot of wet cyclists. But who cares when we're having this much fun. A woman in a swimsuit and wellies stops her bike to make a phone call. On her back a hand-painted sign reads, 'One Less Car'.

Exactly.

It's getting on for eight o'clock, the rain has stopped and I decide to split off on my own before dark. Riding solo around Rome is a lot different than the last four hours. It's a lot faster for a start. But it's that liberated feeling I love the most as I pick up speed and the wind blows against me.

Riding up to Piazza Quirinale, I watch the blazing sun go down, the unmistakable dome of St Peter's on the skyline.

One of the highlights from last year was the immortal Trevi Fountain. It's just downhill and round the corner.

Tonight, it's no less subdued. I lock my bike to a lamppost and work my way through the noisy crowd in the tight piazza.

Down the steps, people sit on the edge flipping coins over their shoulders into the water for a return to Rome or luck in love. Indians with polaroid cameras slung around their necks hustle the tourists for snapshots, a throwback in this era of the selfie. Two policemen watch from the side making sure no one takes a Dolce Vita dip.

But it's all okay. It's the vibe that matters and tonight everyone is in a good mood, again.

The fountain is loud and that's part of the allure. A tiny trickle would just not cut it. It's a statement and Rome is all about statements. Winged horses vault from the cascade, grappled by mermen as Neptune and his two backup singers look on in this massive Baroque spectacle.

It's like being at a rock concert.

Riding back over the Quirinal Hill and down into Monti, I hike the bike up four flights and decompress after a day on two wheels.

The Appian Way

It wouldn't be right if I could not use the bike for one more day. Besides, it's my last day here at Alessia's.

Kitting myself out with sun hat and water, I ride over to the rental shop and make arrangements.

Via Cavour is all downhill as I freewheel towards the Forum on this beautiful day. Turning on Via Imperiali, past the droves of *turisti*, I ride round the Colosseum, past the Palatine Hill on bumpy cobblestones and over to one of the other seven hills of Rome, Monte Celio, the Celian Hill.

Down a narrow street, no cars or houses, high walls either side, I stop at one of the oldest gates defining the boundary of Ancient Rome, the Arco di Dolabella. It's not that imposing, not the usual huge I've become accustomed to, but it still has that powerful sense of history and importance. As I slowly ride through I get the feeling of moving through a portal, a dimension in time.

Past the gate to the right is a delightful park, Villa Celimontana. The ochre-hued villa straight ahead, no longer a family residence, displays a sign of its new owners: Società Geografica Italiana.

Dappled light streams through an avenue of trees; two giant terracotta urns stand before an obelisk, partly hidden; a small fountain gurgles. There's only a few people about which makes me think it's more of a local hangout than a tourist destination, even though it commands panoramic views over the city.

Back on the street, I cruise downhill past a line of parked tour buses and into a very large, very busy intersection. I'm used to this by now and know how to weave through traffic without injury or death. It's all about eye contact, instinct and timing.

Out of the melee and into a quiet neighborhood, the ancient city wall towers beside me as I follow its course. Rome was a very different, much smaller place back then, at least in terms of square miles and population.

An old woman in bright red walks slowly, painfully, through the arch of Porta Latina while a young mother tries to negotiate unsuccessfully with her screaming toddler. The polarities of life show themselves everywhere in Italy.

Further along the wall, I arrive at Porta San Sebastiano, a much larger, much more impressive city gate with a tower either side and a museum inside. It's the start of modern-day Via Appia Antica, Rome's old Appian Way.

Riding through, I find another smaller, older arch from Ancient Rome. Standing underneath it, I'm in that same portal between worlds like so much of Rome. It's one big time machine.

When it was built about 300 B.C., the Appia Antica stretched from the Forum to the trading port of Brindisi, three hundred and fifty miles away on the heel of Italy's boot. The Romans new how to do straight. They also new how to do strong. Given the prodigious amount of potholes in modern tarmac, this two-thousand-year-old stone highway remains intact, proving that older is sometimes better.

Today it extends about ten miles, preserved as a regional park. Riding such a long straight road removes the need for concentration and a certain euphoria arises from pedaling without focus. Even though there's occasional traffic, I'm taking in more of the scenery, the warmth, the wonder. I'm in the zone.

Turning off for a while, I head into the wide-open space of Caffarella Park. On such a glorious day, being away from cars and road noise makes for an even more peaceful, blissful ride.

A serious cyclist covered in corporate branding speeds by on his Bianchi. He's on a mission working up a sweat as I coast along in my sun hat.

Pulling up at what looks like a small temple, I dismount to investigate. A sign tells me this was thought to be a 'temple to Rediculus, God of the Return and Protector of Travelers'. How appropriate. There have been times when I have thought my travels were getting pretty rediculus.

The temple is actually the tomb of Annia Regilla, wife of a wealthy and prominent Greek. The grounds of their villa is what is now Caffarella Park. Knowing this gives me a better sense of context. To truly appreciate Rome, you have to understand its past.

Back in the day, you could not bury anyone inside the city. It was sacred ground. So all the bodies were buried outside the city walls, which makes Via Appia Antica the Road of the Dead.

The remains of tombs and mausoleums stand either side, some in better shape than others, some with the faces of their inhabitants. There are also a number of catacombs, burial chambers that extend for miles underground.

From the outside, the Catacombs of San Callisto seem tranquil with a long avenue of cypress trees, a beautifully landscaped garden and serene statues. But this is just a masquerade for what lies beneath.

I lock my bike and buy a ticket. The pretty face behind the glass offers me a map and some change.

"Grazie, signora."

"Prego," comes the reply with that endearing emphasis.

"*No fotos allaowed*," she warns with another smile and a wave of her finger. I'd be more than happy if you caught me taking a picture.

I walk over to wait with a small group of fellow tourists for the English-speaking guide to arrive.

A large jovial man with a twinkle in his eye appears, and in his Spanish accent, a sudden departure from what I've become used to, bids us to join him.

We enter a slim stone staircase and descend. This is not a place for the claustrophobic—deep, dark and dank with the musty smell of some very old human remains.

This wall-to-wall well-stocked cellar is home to over half a million dead people. And it's not as if they all died a peaceful death, either. Most are the graves of Christians, many slaughtered for their beliefs by the pagan Romans before they themselves converted during the reign of Emperor Constantine. Bad timing to be a Christian.

Our guide's good humor is a welcome relief.

Descending further, we are well below ground—a few stories below. So this is what it feels like to be buried. No Dracula, no zombies, no bread, just darkness and a heavy, oppressive silence, interrupted by our nervous chatter and some atmospheric lighting. But it's that musty odor of a very confined, very old place that makes me yearn for fresh air.

What a difference to my moment of light and emptiness in the Pantheon.

"We can only be here for a maximum of twenty minutes as there is not enough oxygen," our guide calmly informs us, as if it's a game who can survive the longest.

I take a breath of our stale shared air and wonder how

many lungs it has passed through in this macabre intimacy.

During the Sack of Rome in 410, we learn, the catacombs were plundered by barbarians, warring Visigoth tribes from what is now Germany, looting the gold and riches that were buried with their owners.

There must be so many ghosts, so many spirits down here. I haven't met any, but that doesn't mean they're not here. I get that creeping feeling and slowly turn around, catching the eye of a young woman. She really looks like she doesn't want to be here and I offer a comforting if useless smile.

Our jovial guide does a quick head count in case of stragglers or anyone deciding to wander off. There are twelve miles of tunnels down here, no mobile signal and no air, so best not. Everyone accounted for, he directs us back up the steps just in time, making sure we can still breathe.

The first scent of fresh air fills my nose like a breath of heaven. Even though I learned a lot, I had an experience I will never forget.

That relatively short, temporary taste of burial gives me perspective on my mother's long-term fatality: I get to return to life while her body has finished its use, her soul liberated from its mortal coil.

Yet her flesh made my own. Each cell of my body contains her chromosomes. I am a physical continuation of both she and my father. Her body may be gone but she lives on in mine.

This carnal continuum sheds yet more light on my maternal loss.

Back on two wheels, I savor the joys of freedom, fresh air and sunlight as I cruise down the Appian Way, glad to be alive.

The well-placed and aptly titled Caffè dell'Appia Antica beckons me with its outdoor tables.

Sitting in the sun sipping strong espresso, the sign on the trattoria across the way catches my eye: Qui Nun Se More Mai—Roman dialect for, Here One Never Dies. Such Italian humor brings a smile to my face.

The *caffè* kicks in and I'm off.

A group of cyclists head towards me in full regalia with helmets and more corporate branding. But I'm taken by surprise as the leader comes way too close, shouting in my face as he rides by, sticking his leg out to force me off the road. The others laugh and jeer in Italian. I can only guess that this is their idea of having fun, pushing around a tourist, proving to each other how macho they are. It's then I realize I'm on the wrong side of the road. Since when has that ever been a problem in Italy?

But I'm not letting any of this interrupt the joy of my day.

The stones the Romans used to build the Appia Antica are big. On parts of the road, they are so big you can't ride over them and have to use the paths either side. I notice that people on foot and on wheels are using both sides to go in either direction, making the earlier altercation even more unnecessary while proving my point.

Turning into a gravel driveway, I find myself in the gardens of a villa, the Capo di Bove museum. A man in a sharp suit, shades and a shaved head comes out and commands me to dismount. I don't understand his Italian, but I understand his tone.

Yes, sir!

There's not that much to see from the outside, I don't want to pay to visit the architectural remains and I don't feel welcome. What is it with Italians today? Are they just fed up with tourists or do they need to show who's boss? Probably both. Or maybe I'm just not reading the signs.

Back on the Appia Antica, I continue my ride in cycling nirvana. This road is so long and straight, I could ride it forever. Walking it would be a completely different experience—slower, more educational, more connected. Being on two wheels makes it a thrill.

Past more ruined mausoleums inhaling more fresh country air, I reluctantly decide to turn back. It's getting late.

Returning to urban Rome, I'm sharing the road not just with Italian drivers, but Roman drivers. It's not for the faint of heart. You have to be confident and know what you're doing. It's all about flowing with the chaos and keeping your eyes open. Wide open.

Pedaling past the piazza in front of Sant'Anastasia, past the little street that leads down to the Arco di Gaiano, the giant four-way stone arch, the only one of its kind in

Rome, I ride round to a magnificent rear view of the Forum. It's the perfect time to be here as everything begins to glow in the magic hour.

Pushing my bike up the back of the Capitoline Hill, I stop to rest in the Campidoglio.

There's something about this place that keeps pulling me here. Not just Michelangelo's star-shaped floor design, the statue of Emperor Marcus Aurelius on horseback, the elegant porticos of the museums either side—there's something more. It's the ambience of everything together in one cohesive whole: the gentle sound of running water from the fountain overlooked by Minerva, goddess of wisdom and the arts amongst other things; the giant reclining river gods of the Nile and the Tiber either side—it all creates a mythical sense of history, of film sets and Fellini, of something so uniquely Roman.

Cruising down the flat, wide and empty Via dei Fori Imperiali, I turn up Via Cavour to the rental shop. The bike has stayed in great shape and I hand it to smiling faces inside. The cycling community is strong here in Rome as Alessia has shown me, and after today and the Ciemmona yesterday, I feel even more part of it.

It's Not Just About the Food

It's a beautiful sunny morning in Monti and breakfast in the shade overlooking Piazza Madonna puts me on the stage set of Roman life.

Sipping *caffè* at an outdoor table under the canopy of vines, I look out as the day begins. A young woman in a bright yellow dress is a burst of color on the gray *sampietrini* cobblestones; another young woman crosses the piazza, pausing every few paces for her little dog to smell the latest; a man sits by the fountain smoking a cigarette, a smile lighting up his face as his friend arrives.

There's no one over sixty here, at least not this morning. Usually, it's the older generation who share the daily gossip, keeping track of who's who, what they're doing and with whom. Not so easy in Rome.

Monti is the neighborhood for cool people—creative types, artists, writers, hipsters, movers and shakers. It's

Rome's version of New York's Village.

Back at the apartment I finalize travel plans for Napoli and the Amalfi Coast, updating my budget and taking advantage of the internet while I can, another important reminder on the road. Further south may involve more physical connection but internet connection becomes a rarity.

I've applied to as many Couchsurfing hosts in Naples as I could find to no avail. The ones that did reply were either out of town or hosting other people, which means, just as in Florence, I have to switch to Plan B—Plan Airbnb.

I Fiori di Napoli fits the bill with great reviews, an excellent location and a decent price. By now, I'm okay with this. When Couchsurfing doesn't yield results, go with the flow.

I pack the small green carry-on that Alessia lent me, have some lunch and a nap, which by now I've learned is mandatory.

Rome has two metro lines, A and B forming a rudimentary X, with Laurentina at the southwest end of line B. Line C is coming, but it's going to be a while as tunneling under Rome is an archeologist's nightmare.

It's a fairly long trip into the suburbs but I know it's going to be worth it as I'm staying with my very British friend and Couchsurfing host Vicky for a few days before I leave for Naples.

As I ride the train, I can't help but think of the tour of Rome she gave me last year that was filled with laughs and priceless moments.

Vicky waves from the other side of the ticket barrier with that big smile and after hugs and hellos, we take the bus back to her place.

Her spacious top-floor flat has a big terrace where we watch a spectacular sunset over Rome. I can understand why she doesn't want to move.

She's prepared a delicious vegetarian dinner for two, a hearty lentil and veggie stew, *bruschetta* with fresh *pomodoro* drizzled in olive oil and a leafy salad, over which we catch up after not seeing each other since last year.

Vicky is her hilarious self and manages to find wicked humor in just about anything. It's a supremely British trait and one she hasn't given up since moving to Rome. With all the chaos and frustration here, it's kept her sane.

Catching up takes until two in the morning when we're watching Monty Python clips on YouTube. By this point, we're so tired we can't catch up any longer.

After five short hours of sleep and a quick breakfast, Vicky and I head downtown. She's going to teach a class of Italians how to speak English, not the easiest of tasks, while I'm going to meet Alessia and Giangi for lunch.

Leaving Vicky to her educational plight, I take in more of this magical, epic city while I can.

Rome has something indescribable, and as much as I

go on about it, there's a mystery to Rome that is beyond words. But I'll try.

It takes you in its sway. It holds you rapt as if in a dream. It carries you. It holds you close to its bosom. There is an abundance of bosom in Rome, both in flesh and stone, but it's that passionate beating heart of the city I'm alluding to. It's not maternal. Rome makes love to you.

Maybe that's why so many people smoke around here.

Riding the tiny lift up to Alessia's, I hang out with Giangi while we await her return. Giangi was raised in Naples and gives me the lowdown on his hometown.

"Long ago," he tells me, "the three major cities of Europe were St. Petersburg, Paris and Napoli. Each were gateways between regions. Back then, Napoli was a rich and powerful kingdom, but Nelson came over with the British Navy and the rest is history.

"And while you're there, you must go to Nennella's. It's a tiny trattoria that started in someone's living room and then spilled out onto the street."

I like Giangi. He's so down to earth, so full of light and life. He talks about *lo spazio vitale*—the personal space we exist in.

"The mountain people shake hands at a distance. The people in northern towns come a little closer. In Rome, they will touch you. In Naples, they push and jostle you as a normal thing to do."

This is something I will find out very soon. I already had a taste of it in the supermarket in Florence. God knows what it's going to be like in Sicily.

Alessia has put together a lunch for us in her recouped kitchen that is absolutely delicious and didn't cost her a penny. Living a more alternative lifestyle, she is highly resourceful—she has to be. A vegetarian, she reclaims fresh produce from local markets at the end of the day that would otherwise be thrown away. Much of what is discarded is in perfectly good shape and it's a waste not to, for many reasons.

I'm more than impressed and so is Giangi.

It's these moments that makes me realize in Italy, it's not just about the food but about the company you keep. A meal is a social event whether with family or friends, but most likely both. With all the loving care gone into producing, procuring and preparing and the history and tradition involved, it's not something to rush. It's a reason to come together, another opportunity to connect, and Italy is all about connection.

That evening, that connection continues over dinner with Vicky at a local restaurant not far from her flat. The food, although not reclaimed, is also vegetarian, it's good and it's cheap and that's fine with us.

Vicky is a passionate woman about many things, music being one of them. She's a die-hard Peter Gabriel fan and we spend most of the time extolling his virtues, discussing which is his best song (Before The Flood and Don't Give Up tie in first place) before turning to life in

Italy, a conversation that will last much longer than dinner.

She tells of the corruption in Italian government and how life here is fraught with too many rules and an archaic web of bureaucracy that would feel right at home in the twelve miles of catacombs under San Callisto.

With some justified anger in her voice, she relates the despicable way women are treated in Italy, how one woman is killed every three days from domestic violence, and how men who murder women get off lightly; how unfairness seems to be the rule of law in this patriarchal society.

Given the idolization of women, of Italian mothers and the divine mother herself, patriarchy seems a charade to hide the truth that men are deeply threatened by the power women have over them and by their ability to reproduce other men.

She describes the invisible tentacles of the mafia that reach into so much of Italian life, a shadow that never goes away. But that is a whole other book to write.

I'm learning more about the dark side of *la dolce vita.*

Yet somehow, life in Rome continues in its chaotic, passionate momentum. Amidst the shocking realities and statistics, there is still the will to continue, to love, to celebrate the eternal power of being Roman.

Having lived here for thirty years, Vicky is resilient and, like Alessia, resourceful. That strength radiates from her. She's not just a passionate woman, she's a powerful one. She has to be.

Bellies full, musical tastes agreed upon, friendships firmly in place, we head out the door into the warm evening.

The next day is an early start. I take breakfast with Vicky on the terrace and it's already getting hot in the morning sun.

Making the trek out to the suburbs has been beneficial in many ways, not just to see Vicky again, to feel our shared heritage and our love for Rome, but to hear the realities of living here. It's been an education.

But now it's time to go. Armed with just an iPhone and a carry-on, I set off for Naples, the Amalfi Coast and Sicily.

NAPLES

Arrivo
a Napoli

Getting off the train at Napoli Centrale, I head into a new city, a new experience, a new life, even if it's only for a few days.

Walking through the station I look for the information desk. A tall, no-nonsense *carabiniere* holding a submachine gun stands in the middle of the concourse, legs apart, ready for trouble. I walk up to him to ask in my best Italian, but he stops me at my second word with a loud, "*No!*"

Right, then.

Over the concourse, I find the large station map and get my bearings.

A young *napolitana* greets me at the desk with a brief smile. I ask her for an Arte Card, the all-access pass to Napoli and Pompeii. She points out there are five different cards to choose from and would I like this one as the one

I'm after is sold out. I can see her patience wear thin as I weigh my options. I'm just another tourist and her mind is probably elsewhere.

I buy the card for buses and museums, only to discover later that I could have saved money with a different one. Oh, well. With a *grazie*, my card and a map, I'm ready.

Walking into the metro station, I get my first dose of Napoli confusion. The signs for my destination point to two platforms and I have no idea which one. I head down the steps as loud trains pull in. They don't look like metro trains. They look like the train I just took from Rome. Big, dirty, noisy, definitely un–metro like. I look at the signs and then again at my metro map. This has to be the most confusing metro I've ever seen. Unlike the simple two lines in Rome, this is spaghetti.

I approach a fellow traveler for help.

"*Scusi... Montesanto?*" I ask, pointing down the platform.

"*Sì, sì,*" he smiles, pointing in the same direction, my panic dissipating.

The ride is not that long and I exit the station into the busy streets of Naples. The sun begins its afternoon descent, still high enough to make it a hot day. People are everywhere. According to Google Maps, I Fiori di Napoli is down here, turn right and right again.

Right is downhill into a packed street market, the Pignasecca, also recommended by Giangi. The smell of fish is all-pervading. Vendors shout their latest catch, vying for attention with the best price. I pull my small green bag down the cobbled street into the throng, making physical contact on the way. Two girls in shorts, tank tops and helmets slow down to squeeze past on a scooter. I'm back on a movie set filled with extras.

Finally, at the bottom of the hill I reach Via Toledo, a more metropolitan street with wide sidewalks and big shops—and more people.

Napoli is a place of poverty and population, everyone making the best of their economic plight dressed as Italians do and walking with attitude. With this amount of people, I'm reminded of India but with style and cleavage. Then there are the elegant elderly walking amongst the crowd in their finery, unshaken by their context as if from another time. Given this feels like a third-world city, it's a remarkable sight to see this pride in being Neapolitan.

I make a right uphill into the Quartieri Spagnoli, the old Spanish Quarter. It should be just up here on the next block. A scooter rushes by with an inch to spare, the wind blowing my shirt. I go up, I go back down, I turn left. I'm really getting lost here. I take another look at Google Maps to see there are three I Fiori di Napoli in the space of two blocks and my little blue location marker is moving around on its own.

Why does this seem completely appropriate?

Pulling up directions from the email, I try and find where I'm supposed to go. Although they are fairly precise, I'm still getting lost. I stop on the sidewalk in the general vicinity of where I think I'm supposed to be and look around. A man steps out of a doorway beside me with meek eyes and a subdued demeanor, gesturing back inside.

"*I Fiori di Napoli?*" he offers, quietly.

"*Sì. Grazie, signore.*"

As I approach the door, I notice a small handwritten sign hidden above a row of buzzers—I Fiori di Napoli.

I step over the raised threshold and enter a courtyard of storied arches rising above me, each overflowing with greenery, the open roof shedding light down into the space.

Ten flights up—thank God I don't have the Beast—I buzz the door and am greeted with a big smile.

With dark hair, dark eyes and a gentle, low voice, Manuela carries an air of welcoming yet weathered tolerance having to greet and manage so many foreigners and live in a city like Naples.

She shows me to my room and I drop my bags with a sigh of relief and spread out on the bed. Each room has, appropriately, a flower theme decorated with its associated color. I'm in the Dandelion Room. Mellow yellow.

After a change of clothes, I see Manuela in the hallway and she offers me the guided tour—self-service kitchen, dining room, bathroom and up some steep steps, a spacious terrace on the roof.

From this vantage point, the late-afternoon sun casts its golden glow over Naples. The twin peaks of Vesuvius dominate the skyline, these mammaries of magma an ever-present reminder of the fate of neighboring Pompeii.

The roof is decorated with plants, loungers and a table and chairs for outdoor dining. It looks the perfect spot were it not for the cigarette smoke drifting towards me. It appears that smoking is a social imperative in Italy.

Manuela and I go back downstairs and I ask her about Napoli and the surrounds. She tells me that Napoli used to be a wealthy kingdom that you can still see traces of today. It was the main trading port of the Mediterranean and along with Paris and St. Petersburg formed a triangle of the wealthiest and most important cities in Europe—just as Giangi told me.

Napoli is in the region of Campania, famous for its beautiful coastline and seafood. It's the Riviera Napoletana. Napoli is also home to the Comorra, a group of violent clans that control its streets, or at least used to.

"I've heard some bad things about Naples. Are there places I shouldn't go?" I ask her.

"Poor little boy," she replies, a wry smile softening the sarcasm.

Light on
the Piazza

Liberated of luggage, I descend the ten flights of stairs with just a set of keys, my wallet and my phone. Out on the street, scooters rush by again. I feel like I live here, if only for a few days. That delusion gives me a confident stride, taking me past the enticing aromas of Caffè Rosati and Caffè Gambrinus on Via Toledo, but it's way too late in the day for that and I continue on towards the harbor.

Via Toledo ends at the grand Piazza del Plebiscito. Along the far side of this wide empty space stands San Francesco da Paola, a round basilica reminiscent of the Pantheon with its classical portico and two extra domes, while its curved colonnades extend either side like arms embracing the piazza. Some teenage girls stand in the middle, filling the air with laughter; boys chase each other at one end; people sit among the columns watching the changing light.

All this space is such a paradox to the rest of Naples.

The sun casts its magical glow over the piazza as I make my way to the water, the deep red ochre of Palazzo Reale aflame with color as boats glisten on dark blue. Above it all, the magmammaries of Vesuvius curve the skyline with ominous grace.

Warm evenings such as this are a joy, a haven for my system. I feel myself let go inside, the sea breeze gently caressing my skin.

"Oh, thank you," I whisper. Once again, I feel blessed.

Across the piazza, the sun silhouettes the angular shapes of Castel Sant'Elmo high above Naples atop Vomero Hill, my destination tomorrow.

But now it's time for food and I know where I'm headed.

The Avocado

As twilight begins and lights flicker, nightlife comes alive in the narrow streets of the Quartieri Spagnoli. Small multicolored flags hang between the tall tightly-packed buildings along with the laundry. I feel like I've wandered into another world, another time. More scooters rush by.

I pass a row of dumpsters overflowing with trash. The mafia run the utilities and clearly they're not motivated to clean up. Either payments are late or they just don't care. Knowing a little of the Italian ways, I'd go for a combination of both. It's only later I hear that they don't have anywhere to put it. Italian landfills are full and the costs of shipping trash to other countries has gone up. Some countries won't take Italy's trash at all. There's more to this than meets the eye.

The tables of Trattoria da Nennella, as Giangi told me, spread into the street covered by an awning. There's just enough room between the cordoning rope and the opposite building for pedestrians to squeeze by, but most definitely not a car. Not even a Cinquecento. The police don't seem to mind this infraction of a thoroughfare. I doubt the police venture up here much at all except for off-duty dinner or an off-duty something.

A moped revs up, awkwardly navigating the tiny passage full of people, swimming upstream.

I get pointed to a table by a very large waiter in a white t-shirt and an apron rolled down to his middle. He smiles briefly and hands me a photocopied handwritten menu with today's dishes. I decide on some fish and place my order, which he shouts into the kitchen with a booming voice, throwing a basket of bread in front of me while shouting more Italian to summon customers. This is fun.

Another very large man in a smart green open-neck shirt walks between the tables, catches my eye and motions to the seat next to me.

"Posso?" he asks.

"*Sì, sì,*" I return, moving my chair so he can sit down.

His smile spends more time on his face than the waiter's and we start up a conversation, my stumbling Italian and his broken English.

He asks me about women, of course, and I tell him about the beautiful ladies of Denmark. He grimaces.

"North Europe women, they are so hard. They take-a your balls and not give them back."

I manage a concerned look and contemplate the

possibility of his statement.

"*South Italian women, aah…*" His smile spreads wider. "*Napolitana and Sitchiliana women are soooo sweet. They will love you! Just love them back… or they will kill you.*" His smile disappears for a truthful moment before he bursts into laughter.

With another concerned look, I contemplate the possibility of his new statement.

I ask his line of work.

"*Avocado,*" he tells me. What? Is he a grocer? A farmer? He looks too clean for that.

"Avocado?" I ask.

"*Sì, I am a creeminal justice lawyer. Un avvocato.*"

I look at him for a moment longer than usual and it strikes me this man does not represent the innocent.

He tells me he's from Messina, the most beautiful city in Sicilia, I'm assured.

Sicily. Of course.

We finish the simple authentic meal and our conversation and get up to pay.

At that moment, something goes down at the entrance. Two men arrive and commandeer the register, one with a thick wad of Euros. As we approach them, the Avocado asks for my money.

After a moment's hesitation I decide there is no option but to hand over my €50. He speaks to the men in loud Italian and they exchange money, counting each note.

Stepping out into the street, he gives me my change

and confirms my instinct, asking if I want to take a walk and get some gelato.

I start to worry. I'm in Naples in the dark with a very large criminal lawyer who just made a nefarious transaction with my money. I politely decline, but he presses on and asks for my mobile number. I tell him I have to make a call to my North Europe hardlady. He smiles, but I can't help feel he could snap me like a twig if he so desired.

I briefly contemplate possible outcomes of our shared gelato and phone numbers and arrive at sodomy, mutilation and concrete.

He extends a hand and we shake. This is a firm handshake. So firm, the twig option is getting closer, but he lets go and waves as he walks away.

I head back to I Fiori and see another side street overflowing with trash.

Viva Napoli.

Taking Vomero Hill

In the breakfast room of I Fiori di Napoli, a large spread of cereal, pastries, fruit and coffee fills the table. Sitting opposite me is a young man with blond hair in a purple lamé shirt, an American it turns out from Connecticut. He tells me of his impending trip to Capri and we share some travel tales before he leaves for the harbor.

Today, I will not be going to Capri, although that is a wonderful thought. Island of the rich and famous, Bond location and spot for expensive lounging, Capri—along with Ischia and Procida, though much different—are worth at least one visit across the azure waters the Mediterranean.

Today, I'm headed for a castle.

The noise and the smell of fish in the Pignasecca are overwhelming in the heat of the day, an assault on the senses like so much of Napoli. I keep moving, the tumble of tourists, locals and vendors giving me traction as I work my way back uphill to Montesanto station, trying my best to avoid passing scooters on their way down.

Buying tickets in Italy is second nature to me now as I operate the red Trenitalia machine, its charming voice warning me of *peek pockets* more apt here than anywhere.

On the main concourse, two tunnels open up onto four platforms where people are either waiting, coming or going.

I follow the sign to the *funicolare* as a woman in a tight black dress steps in front of me, her bare legs worked out, heels clicking.

Women lead the way, figuratively and literally, however much men feel in control. The feminine in all her forms have graced the prows of ships, have been queens and courtesans, mothers and wives, or in my case, fellow passengers, to bring the awe-struck male towards his destination.

But this isn't just about physical attraction, it's a deeper primal instinct, a knowing that women carry the race, that nourish. That without them, we would be lost, adrift. The Italian veneration for the mother and grandmother seems a natural expression of this profound human need.

As if on cue, an older woman with a small child, *nonna* and *nipotina*, looks for a place in the carriage; a respectable man in his sixties wearing a tan fedora takes a seat; two young dudes in shades climb in. Observing this cross-section of Neapolitan life, I feel for a moment how it would be to belong here.

The *funicolare* starts its chain-geared ride uphill. We're all sitting backwards, the stadium seating providing a spectacular view of Naples on our way to the top. More of an amusement ride than a train, I want to ride it a few times before getting out.

Vomero is a very different neighborhood than the rest of Napoli, so much so it could be a different city, more European, light and airy with hardly any traffic. Leafy streets open up to commanding views over the densely populated chaos below, a reminder of where we are.

Looking down from this peace and tranquility, you can't help but feel Naples is a threatening place, its bloody history giving it a violent charisma. The sense of survival is in the air and on the streets. But the people of Naples have survived volcanos, earthquakes, warfare, cholera and the mafia and still manage to laugh, sing, make babies and pizza. It's what gives Naples its pulse and passion.

Castel Sant'Elmo is a powerful sight, its fortifications rising up to make one feel small and helpless, as intended. There's no way anyone could break this down, which is probably why it's still here. Seen from the air, it's built in an elongated star shape, its battlements an angular contrast to the curvaceous Vesuvio across the bay.

Inside the castle grounds I walk up to the ticket window. Two men lean back in their rolling chairs talking, ignoring me. One of them slides over to the window.

"*Dieci Euro,*" he says, continuing the conversation with

his friend.

I give him the money without so much as a *prego* in return—something else I'm getting used to in Italy.

Approaching this giant edifice, ticket in hand, I feel smaller with every step. I imagine battles and sieges and human strife, but that's all gone now, at least up here. What's left is a presence, an energy.

I find the entrance and step into the sudden cool of an elevator. Going up, it gradually slows to a halt as the doors slide open and the heat hits me.

I'm on a movie set again. Everything about Italy is drama—the skies, the opera, the art, the people, and this is no exception. Where once an army assembled is now a vast empty space. I make my way towards the parapet and walk the entire star-shaped perimeter, an Englishman out in the midday sun, minus the dogs.

There are only two other people here, probably English as well. Everyone else is inside. Call me barking mad, but I'm getting the full experience and the view across the Bay of Naples is breathtaking. This is a supreme vantage point, regardless of history or heat.

The sprawling city laid out before me begs for a photograph. Actually, it begs for Sophia Loren and a film crew, but that's not going to happen so I press on around the parapet.

It's hot. Very hot. And I don't have any water with me. I reach the halfway point and look over the wall into the drop of death. It's a very, very, very long way down and dehydration is setting in.

Can I fly? Should I try? No. Stop that.

The whole place is beginning to feel like a dream.

Paladino's sculpture of a giant infantry helmet with long protruding spines interrupts the view, a reminder why this place was built. I feel myself going back in time as my dream becomes real.

I'd better find some shade, fast. Stepping into a tent-like structure built especially for this purpose, I'm just sitting in a makeshift oven.

Back outside I see the entrance to a gallery. Four men sit inside talking. They glance at me, nodding. Meandering through the gallery, I start to cool down, although cool is not strictly accurate. It's just not hell hot.

The paintings are all modern works, the Italian drama once again on display. I wander from room to room, studying these expressions of creativity.

A large triptych depicts a group of naked women flanked by two naked men, all with their hands raised in some kind of dance. They stand on a hill overlooking an island, Ischia is my guess, their faces a mixture of joy and horror, an accurate portrayal of life in Naples.

Descending in the cool of the elevator, I enjoy a minute's respite.

A vintage light-blue Cinquecento greets me at the sidewalk. If I only had the keys… a fantasy that lasts but a few short seconds as I imagine driving in Napoli where stop lights and signposts are mere suggestions.

Dolls, Dead Monks
and a Donkey

By now I'm totally parched. I find a sidewalk table in the shade and the young waitress comes out to take my order.

"Una granita al limone, per favore," I manage.

This has to be one of my favorite drinks south of Rome. The heat just begs for it, the ice, lemon and sugar blended to perfection. I sit and gaze out over Naples with my *granita* and sunglasses and feel like a movie star.

So this is what it's like to be Italian.

I pay the bill and venture down the Largo. There's not much going on here and I'm the only one about, probably because none of the locals are stupid enough to be out in this heat. The Museo di San Martino is supposed to be down here, but it's hard to find. A small sign above a small door off the piazza announces its location, as if it's trying to hide.

Inside, it all looks a bit boring. Some books, some

display cases and in the corner, a life-size replica of the manger with Mary, Joseph, baby Jesus and a donkey.

A smartly-dressed pretty young woman—are there any ugly people in Italy?—informs me I need to buy a ticket. Paying her the money, she motions towards the door where the donkey is pointing, as if he, too, wants to escape his boredom.

Through the door, I am met with another experience altogether.

The Certosa di San Martino is an old monastery with cloisters around a square garden. Human skulls decorate the garden at strategic points as if to instil the fear of death or God or both. It's the cemetery of the monks, reminding themselves, and us, that life is temporary.

Strolling through open porticos I look up, the faded yellow ochre of the building in vivid contrast against the azure sky. I imagine monks walking through the cloisters —but it's just as easy to imagine couture-clad models posing for a Versace shoot.

Stepping inside, stunning frescos decorate the walls and ceilings. Shafts of sunlight illuminate these masterpieces as if waiting for me, the dance of sun on pigment a reminder of the elemental power of art.

Some rooms are off limits and I step over a rope to take a closer look. Inside are more frescos, this time in a state of renovation covered by scaffolding.

However non-religious, I have a profound, deeply personal relationship with the divine. Being in Italy surrounded by Catholicism, I am in awe at the devotion expressed in art and architecture. Take out the organization and the dogma and you have the artist's pure love of God.

Leaving the Certosa, I head back into the museum via another door and arrive inside a theater. On stage, people are in various moments of dramatic action, except they're not moving. No, they're not the dead monks, they are depicting a scene from a *commedia dell'arte* of Pulcinella, the spaghetti-eating clown. It's eerie to see these life-size, lifelike dolls in total silence, frozen in time.

Exiting stage right, I discover another scene of static sculpted people, this time in miniature. The nativity is depicted in minute detail with tiny characters you could find in real-life Naples involved around the central scene. The craftsmanship is astonishing.

In a cavern behind glass is the famous Cuciniello Crib, a grander, more detailed nativity involving even more tiny Neapolitans with tiny angels descending from heaven.

But however exquisite the display, I've had enough of dolls.

Passing a rather dusty ornate royal carriage, a leftover from this once-Kingdom, I head out into bright sunshine. A terrace leads to a garden and more breathtaking views over the Bay of Naples.

This is what I came for.

Spaccanapoli

Under a covered footpath are tables and chairs posing as a restaurant. It's actually the path to another house, but this being Napoli everyone is comfortable with close proximity.

Its only customer, I take a seat and order my usual budget-friendly *panino e acqua frizzante* from the waiter. Meanwhile, the door of the house opens and a large dog, a ridgeback, followed by his large well-dressed owner squeeze past me to the street. He must be okay with this, but it's a bit odd to have this obstacle course outside your front door.

After what seems an eternity, my sandwich arrives. It amazes me how something so simple can take so long and still taste so good. I want to reprimand the waiter but my tastebuds prevent me.

Digesting the last morsel, I try to pay but the waiter has gone on vacation. I go down some steps into a basement and there he is with two girls and an older woman, his mother most likely, eating together around a table. So that's why my *panino* took so long.

"*Posso pagarlo?*" I ask, waving some Euros.

The waiter turns and shouts behind him. A sweaty cook in a dirty apron emerges with a big smile and shouts back at the waiter, who then gets up and takes my money.

I love Italians. They don't hold their tongue or anything else for that matter. All the shouting and waving has one simple objective—to connect.

Wandering slowly back to the *funicolare*, I enjoy this privileged sense of space high above the city, before descending back into the density and drama below.

Sitting in the strange little train, the ride down is just as much fun as the ride up.

There's still a few hours of daylight left and I decide to take a walk through the *centro storico*, the historical center. But I did not account for the fact that a) it's still really hot, and b) I need a nap.

The street is long, much longer than it appears on the map. It's Spaccanapoli, the road that cuts Napoli in half made when the Greeks first created Neapolis. I stop at a spigot and wet the back of my neck.

Both Giangi and Manuela recommended I visit this area, home to some of the great works including Sanmartino's Veiled Christ, supposedly the most moving portrayal ever made, and those of the rebel genius and my personal favorite, Caravaggio.

As I stand with cool water dripping down my back, I see the monumental door of the Chiesa del Gesù Nuovo across the street. Surrounded by dark pointed masonry that covers the front of the building, it looks more like a fortress than a church and captures the brutal paradox of medieval Catholicism—the glory and grandeur of salvation along with some murderous torture.

Walking down this long, perfectly straight thoroughfare, wares spilling out from tiny shops either side, the bustling flow of people in both directions, I feel I'm in the beating heart of Naples.

A large piazza opens up to one side, an ornate obelisk rising up in the center; a giant crane holds a camera; workers in black move equipment while fans watch a chef in white prepare a meal in a kitchen created in the square. They're shooting an episode of Master Chef and while it's fun to see the hoopla, I'm more interested in the history of this incredible city.

Tucked into a side street, a statue of the reclining river god Nilo stares at me, holding his cornucopia of plenty. It's as if he's saying, 'Life is an abundant overflow of riches. You'll always have more than enough. Just look at the stream of humanity flowing all around you!'

This message, however much my own interpretation, strikes deep, a reminder of the truth of life whenever I'm caught in limiting thoughts of lack and not having enough.

Looking down the endless Spaccanapoli, I contemplate

further exploration. Except if I don't stop walking I'm going to collapse. No Caravaggio, no Veiled Christ, not today. I turn around and head back, past the show, past the gift shops, past a hair salon.

Wait! A hair salon—that means sitting down in air conditioning. Okay, I'm going to get styled.

Entering the cool of Bassani Space, I am greeted by Alessandro, a charming young man who speaks a little English. He calls over his boss and we get introduced. His English is much better and I tell him what I want before he motions me to sit down, translating my wishes to Alessandro.

A pretty assistant with dark eyes and firm hands shampoos me over a sink and then massages my head for ten minutes with tingling menthol, her strong fingers pushing and pulling out the exhaustion of the day. This is heaven.

Back in the big leather barber's chair, Alessandro is ready and begins to dance around me, lifting, twirling, snipping, blowing and more snipping to create his masterpiece. I feel I'm in the hands of an artist.

After about thirty minutes of this, accompanied by hypnotic background beats on the sound system, he holds up a mirror for my inspection. I'm impressed. No, I'm overjoyed.

Finally, he infuses my hair with a product, but not just any product. This is the magic ingredient, he tells me—Davine's Oil Non Oil. I'll buy it, whatever it is. I feel thoroughly refreshed, styled and very Italian.

Leaving the cool of the air conditioning, I utter praises in the best *italiano* I can muster and take a slow, satisfied walk back to I Fiori.

By the time I get to Via Toledo, the *passeggiata* has begun and I'm blending in a lot more, however illusory that may be. My new coiffure and confidence certainly gets me some looks and the occasional smile. Is that all it takes? I really have to do this more often.

Finding
Valeria

I had already booked I Fiori di Napoli by the time Valeria answered my Couchsurfing request to stay with her. Even though last-minute timing is one of the risks involved, tonight it's no problem. I'm meeting her for dinner with my new hair.

Successfully navigating the spaghetti metro to her stop, this is where the fun begins. I have her address and I've found the street on the map and in real life. I follow the house numbers descending to the right one—except it's not there. Of course it's not there. This is Italy. I should know this by now, but it still catches me out.

I go up and back down the hill and I'm lost again. It's rush hour, it's loud and the fumes are choking me. I stop and call Valeria, my free hand covering the side of the phone as I jam it up against my face. I can just about hear her Italian-English directions.

"Walk to the *piccola piazza* downhill."

As I walk to the small *piazzetta*, my phone rings again.

"Navyo! I see you! Up here. On the balcony. No, to your left."

I look up across the street and see her wave, pointing down to a door. I walk directly into the traffic, the only way to cross a busy street in Naples or Rome, which miraculously lets me pass. I learned this from Giangi, otherwise I'd be waiting all night.

She ushers me in with a kiss on both cheeks.

Upstairs, I am in the home of a professional, furnished for a mix of living and working, the residue of focused activity lingering in the space.

Valeria runs a news photo agency and is used to the pressure of hard deadlines. Amidst the images of homicides and life on the street there is a feminine grace to her. In her exuberant cigarette-growl laugh is the infectious spirit of a passionate *napolitana*. She clearly loves life and is face to face with it every day.

We go out on the balcony where dinner is served. She has made a wonderful spread of fresh fish, grilled vegetables, traditional cheeses and the prerequisite bread and olive oil. It's absolutely delicious and reminds me once again how Couchsurfing is such a positive antidote to the fear of strangers—a network of people around the world who share their lives and homes in the spirit of generosity and connection.

Valeria is someone I feel I've known before. Even

though she has a tough side—who wouldn't in Naples—I can tell there's a tender woman in there.

Sitting out here in the warm evening together, I feel another rush of love for Italy and its people.

Sex in the
Museum

I wake up the next morning exhausted. But it's another day in Naples and I'm not going to let tiredness get in the way of pizza, statues and new friends.

A shower freshens me up and before you know it, it's time to hit the *marciapiede*.

The Museo Archeologico has its own metro stop, Museo. Inside, the station is decorated with images from the museum in shadowplay as if they've come to life. In a large atrium before the exit stands a replica of the ten-foot Hercules, looking as exhausted as me after a day in Naples. Another replica, the Laocoön and his Two Sons being killed by long sinuous serpents adds a warm touch to the morning.

The museum is as grand as its contents with a huge central staircase leading up to more galleries. The stories from the ancient world are not only stirring but, as I'll find out, sexy as well.

As I've seen throughout Italy, Italians love their bodies and have no problem displaying them in art or flesh. The physical body, the very appreciation of it, is a form of social currency where beauty and attraction are used in the transactions of everyday life. It's as if the entire country is flirting with itself.

This social currency can be translated as *bella figura* and its converse, *brutta figura*. Both of these principles are not just about how you dress or what you reveal but how you behave and what you say.

Here in the museum it's much more carnal.

One piece particularly catches my attention—The Group With The Torment Of Dirce, otherwise known as the Farnese Bull, sculpted from just one piece of marble weighing fifteen tons, the largest surviving single sculpture from antiquity.

It's a Roman copy of an original Greek statue, dug up at the Caracalla Baths in Rome back in the 16th century and was meant to adorn the Palazzo Farnese, hence the name.

Two naked brothers wrestle a bull, tying the bare-breasted Dirce, wife of the King of Thebes, underneath to be trampled as punishment for persecuting their mother, who oversees the occasion fully clothed while a young boy and his dog look on.

The men's dangling apparatus are at eye level for the rest of us watching. Especially so for a group of young

American students, all female, who take notes and sketches while their teacher describes the history of the scene.

I can't help but smile.

I continue my tour up the grand staircase to find a large mosaic head of the snake-haired Medusa, her wild stone-turning eyes staring in the direction of a somewhat hidden wrought-iron gate. A sign warns me of explicit images in the Gabinetto Segreto, the Secret Room, containing a collection of erotica from that ill-fated victim of Vesuvius, Pompeii.

Inside, a glass case houses various statuettes worshipping the phallus—small monks with giant erections protruding from their habits; a small man with a phallus larger than himself, plus a number of phalli sprouting from his hat; a large erection with legs and feet and another protrusion beneath; a curved flying penis with wings and little bells dangling from wires.

What were these for, I wonder? Were they put to use by the women of Pompeii? Or was this just Pompeiian pornography?

As I discover, they were given as gifts to be hung on the front door or used as wind chimes to ward off evil spirits and bring fertility, good luck and overall goodness to the home.

I can't think of a more charming, positive family-friendly use of the penis. The pagan humor of it all diffuses the modern social stigma of man's most sensitive part as an unwanted seed dispenser or sexual weapon.

In another room, dark with soft lighting, are paintings of various scenes of carnal pleasure. I survey these acts of love, imagining their historical context, when suddenly I see her. In the corner, in the shadows, is one of the American students furiously sketching. I sense her embarrassment at being discovered and turn away. It's that forbidden ritual on display she wants to take home and show her friends.

Such a regular and natural human activity, yet we still have such shame around it, labeling it an obscenity. It still has to be presented in a darkened room with a warning sign. In religious terms, it's been a sin for centuries and there lies the root of the problem. Isn't it time we woke up from this twisted belief and celebrated the joy of our bodies without guilt?

It seems the Italians are at least trying.

I slowly make my way out of this massive museum and back into the heat of Napoli.

On the other side of the wide, busy street are tables and chairs and a hot display case full of a world-famous creation invented right here in Naples—fresh wood-fired pizza. I am greeted by the gruff voice of the waiter, tired of tourists but nevertheless in their service as money is money. I order a *margherita*, the most widely consumed pizza in Napoli, named after Queen Margherita of Spain when she visited in 1889, although its origins came long before.

The waiter presents this hot fragrant joy and my mouth

can't stop eating it. This is the redemption I've been waiting for. This is the real thing. The melted mozzarella, the *pomodoro*, the fresh *basilico*, the perfect crust—it all keeps seducing my tastebuds for more.

I'm having oral sex with a pizza.

Limoncello
Yellow

The Circumvesuviana, as its name suggests, is the train that goes around Vesuvius to get to Herculanium, Pompeii and Sorrento. The walk inside Stazione Centrale to get to the Circumvesuviana platform is as long as its name and the perfect opportunity to work off my pizza.

Overheated tourists and commuting locals fill the station and everyone looks a little disheveled by two o'clock. Understandably, as it's national nap time. I wait and wait, trying not to fall asleep. Finally, the train arrives and away we go. The wrong way.

I get off at the first stop and wait for the next train back to Stazione Centrale.

By this point, the romance of Naples has lost some of its glamour and I'm tired of the heat and trains and the spaghetti Metro and pollution and scooters and trash and tourists. But I'm still in Italy and I've just had some real

Neapolitan pizza.

I get on the train, direction Sorrento, and my frustration begins to lift.

Trains have a special magic—the motion, the sound, the world rushing by. Riding a train is romantic. It doesn't have to be the Eurostar or the Paris-Milan TGV I took last year. It can be an old *regionale* like this one. It's just that it's a train and I'm being carried along in this shared experience of going somewhere.

The scenery begins to change as we leave the urban sprawl of Naples and follow the rugged Campania coastline south.

Arriving in Sorrento, it's a short walk from the station into town with signs for pensions, hotels and gelato dotting the route. Gone are the trash and pollution. There are tourists of course, but the vibe is completely different. This is not Naples, but then nothing is like Naples.

In the clifftop gardens of Villa Comunale, I walk over to the wall and look down. Tiny people lie tanning in the sun below, others float on loungers, little dots on the clear green water. Along the harbor, palm trees and pastel-hued villas perch on the cliff as the sun-drenched coastline protrudes into the Mediterranean.

Behind me, the convent of San Francesco pulls me in, a welcome change of temperature. The interior is simple and elegant but not ornate. Through a door at the back is another matter, another world, a Sorrento long ago.

Draped in ivy and climbing vines, history etched in its

weathered stone, this place is a dream. Cloisters surround a tree in the central garden, a type of willow perhaps, its hanging foliage relaxed in the sun. I take a slow, tempered walk in the shade and sense the purpose of this place—devotion, contemplation, a little exercise maybe.

Surprisingly, I'm the only one here. The gift of solitude brings such rewards.

Outside, I'm back in the noise of life in Sorrento—young couples pushing strollers, children with oversized cones of gelato, young women dressed for attention, husbands, wives, mothers, grandmothers, tourists. Everyone is out today.

An older lady in a yellow dress and a straw hat covered in flowers—she must be British—gracefully cycles past me, ringing her bell with a smile.

The pink and yellow campanile of the Duomo stands at the end of a narrow street, its colorful focal point. Occupying the corner, a mosaic dome is supported by open arches on two sides. Its interior is covered with aging yet detailed frescos, one wall a scene in diminishing perspective to enlarge the space.

Men, all past middle age, sit at tables under the dome playing cards for all to see like a theatrical performance—not unusual as all life in Italy is theater. There's a clear absence of women, another moment of observing Italian tradition and social order. A sign tells me this is the Società Operaia, the local worker's club. I'm sure the women have a club of their own.

Over another wall is an unexpected sight. Down a sheer vertical drop into a steep gorge stand the ruins of a long-abandoned mill surrounded by trees, their branches invading its crumbling space. It's a haunting scene, one I imagine has already inspired a gothic novel or two.

I look for an entrance to climb down but find nothing.

In contrast, the narrow shopping streets above brim with life, color and local wares, an inordinate amount of fresh lemons, lemon *sorbetto* and the famed *limoncello*. Lemons are everywhere and the scent of their blossom fills the air.

What with intoxicating fragrance, alcohol, a stunning coastline and a haunted ruin, it's no wonder that famous writers came here—Byron, Keats, Goethe, Ibsen and Scott to name a few.

I stop for gelato, lemon of course, and cool down.

I'm hearing a lot of English spoken in Sorrento and am reminded once more of the Grand Tour we Brits used to take in previous centuries, rites of passage through Italy absorbing the culture, winding up here on the Neapolitan Riviera.

The tourists of that era were of a very different breed and took the whole thing to another level, spending years studying and patronizing the arts and getting an education in the process. As well as lots of sex.

More and more, I realize I am on my own Grand Tour —minus the sex, at least for now. My love for Italy overflows in abundance. I could stay in Sorrento for years and immerse myself and write.

As much as that appeals, I can't stay that long, not yet at least.

Postcard Positano

The bus ride from Sorrento to Positano is a life-threatening experience. The driver takes risks that make Formula One look like a ride to the shops. The only thing to trust is that he knows this route like the back of his hand. Tunnel roofs are missed by less than an inch. Curves are taken at velocity and the drop down to the rocks below leaves no room for error. There are *Oooohs* and *Ohhhhs* from the passengers as he throws us around each bend. He's also driving one handed as the other is fixed to the horn, mostly for tourists driving sensibly.

He picks up his mobile and makes a call. I feel myself shrink into the seat and consider holding someone's hand. Suddenly, he shouts at a driver ahead while shaking his phone, then resumes talking. Before we enter the next tunnel, he's back on the horn and I start breathing again.

Waving at oncoming buses as they pass within a hair's

breadth, he yells out the window to his suicidal cohorts in rapid Italian. Maybe they've placed bets on who gets the most runs today—or who escapes a grisly death.

A hot-shot on a Ducati zooms past. I watch him take the curves ahead, risking his life for the thrill of speed on the Riviera Napoletana. But he's not alone. There must be at least five or six aces buzzing by like angry gnats on steroids. I'm starting to think the bus driver has a Ducati at home and this is his practice run.

But however reckless he may be, this stain-inducing rollercoaster is giving us a series of ever-evolving spectacular views.

Positano is another real-life Italian postcard. With mountains providing shelter and spectacle, the pastel colors of this coastal resort built into the cliffs are worthy of every picture. There's a dreamlike quality that inspires not only writers but artists, movie sets and working on a tan.

The bus drops me off at the top of the hill and I wend my way down. There is a local bus that will take me, but I don't want to miss a step on this walk into paradise. Here is that lazy Italian vibe, a few locals standing around chatting, the occasional car, and *le belle donne*. It's as if people don't have a care in the world aside from what to wear and what to eat.

Like Sorrento, it's not as hot as Napoli, the Mediterranean breeze affording some natural air conditioning. I pass the Hotel Royal Positano commanding the view and imagine a few nights of luxury. As I reach more of the town, I see it's going to be a long, hot walk down to the beach. A young girl in a swimsuit with wet hair and a towel round her shoulders comes up some hidden steps and I decide to go down.

Another wet girl passes me, out of breath, yelling up to her friend to wait. At the bottom of the steps, trees provide some needed shade and there's no one else about. I've found a secret passageway completely sheltered and quiet. A creek runs through some rocks down to the sea.

Walking under a bridge, I arrive at a tiny street of houses with open front doors, an empty chair outside each one. An old woman sits presiding over some locals discussing today's catch with a man on the bridge above. He shouts over and throws down a sack of fish.

Coming back onto the main street, I am met with an overflow of *turisti*. This is a different Positano than I saw from above. This is the reality Italians tire of, but it's their income and it's what makes this town run.

As lemons are to Sorrento, so blue hand-painted scarves and ceramics are to Positano. I step inside a shop filled with billowing blue silk draped from the ceiling. Surrounded by color, it's as though I've entered a stage production. Soft silk brushes against my face with a delicate caress as I move around the displays. I feel the urge to close my eyes. The shopkeeper and his wife watch me with wide knowing grins, as if waiting for me to burst into song.

Quietly exiting the shop in a somewhat altered state, I attempt to make my way down to the beach, becoming more of a human sardine as beachgoers fill the tiny streets in both directions.

Making my escape back uphill, the horde gradually thins and I return to the calmer, suave Positano of my postcard. Get the timing right next season and stay a few nights. Work on that tan.

Amalfi:
Men in Tights

With no change of underwear, the bus to Amalfi is another death ride to paradise. At this point, I've stopped caring. I've learned to trust these crazy Italians and the flow of chaos.

This time there's no hill to walk down, no stroll into town. We're dropped off right at the harbor.

At first I'm a bit underwhelmed, but as I explore I realize the history, the uniqueness of the place. It may not be as postcard as Positano but it has the crumbling elegance of Italian beauty that enraptures not just me but the entire world.

Through an archway, it's not the sight but the sound that gets my attention—drums. And horns.

By the time I get to the piazza, the musicians have stopped playing. Up a grand flight of steps the Duomo looms high over the piazza, too large for such a small town. Then I remember Manuela telling me at one time Amalfi was a bigger port than Naples until a tidal wave changed everything.

The musicians, all in traditional costume, line the steps, waiting. I walk up through the crowd for a better view. At the top, the door of the Duomo is open and I peek inside.

Rows of chandeliers illuminate the space, full of atmosphere and well-dressed people. I'm not sure if this is mass, a wedding or some kind of civic blessing. Not wanting to interrupt, I step back out.

The ceremony complete, the well-dressed people and the priest make their way out, the crowd parting as they slowly parade down the steps. Horns fanfare, drums follow. Something's clearly about to happen.

Down on the piazza, men in tights and colored silk circle up with giant flags. In San Francisco, this would be Gay Pride. Here in Italy, it's history, their medieval costumes representing the guilds of the time.

Up on the steps, the drums are played by both men and women—a modern touch to the historical proceedings. Throw in the horns and this is loud.

One costumed performer steps out alone and throws first one, then two flags to rooftop level. Now four. This is getting serious, the crowd cheering with every catch. Soon the entire group are throwing all they've got and not one flag hits the ground.

Drums, horns, flags, tights—it's a spectacle kept alive

since the Middle Ages. I can't believe what a moment I've arrived in. Talk about timing.

Wrapping up to wild applause and shouts of '*Bravi!*', everyone starts to mingle while I take a slow hike up the busy main street in search of food.

The *ristoranti* are not cheap around here, but I manage to find an inexpensive spot and order not one but two medium-sized pizzas. My appetite has the better of me.

But this is when things start to go awry. The girl behind the counter does something no Italian should ever do—she microwaves the pizzas. Did your mother not teach you anything about cooking?

Slowly, unfortunately, I bite into my soft, dead, chewy pizza, not because I'm in Italy, the home of pizza and the best food in the world, but because I'm starving. I feel betrayed and want to cry.

Tolerating misgivings is part of being a visitor to Italy and, so I understand, to being Italian. The more I lower my expectations and go with the flow, the better things get, then exquisite moments suddenly light up like beacons in this tumultuous romance of a country.

Out along the stone pier, I take in the panorama of Amalfi. Rugged mountains silhouette the skyline as the ruins of a castle overlook the sea. Secret villas dot the hills telling me there is more to this place than meets the eye. Boats leave whitewater wakes, colors glisten as the low sun casts its golden light and I feel once again the unmistakable magic of being in Italy.

Stranded
in Sorrento

The life-threatening bus ride back to Sorrento is now a normal occurrence and I enjoy this brush with death in style. If I am to die now, this is the place. But I have a train to catch so better wait.

Arriving at the station, I walk towards the entrance to see a janitor mopping the floor who, with a dismissing wave, lets me know the station is closed.

Now I'm stranded in Sorrento with just my iPhone, my wallet and my wits. But instead of panicking, I find myself smiling. Moments like these are part of the adventure.

I search the web for buses to Napoli and bingo—the very last bus stops right here in about two hours and gets into Napoli at 1 a.m. This has definitely become exciting.

I take a stroll back into town as lights come on and twilight fades. Wandering through the tiny streets with

197

candlelit tables, the fragrance of lemon blossom intoxicates this warm evening and I don't want to leave. Once more, I feel like I am in a dream.

Heading back to the station, my stride slows to a saunter as I relax from a long day on the Riviera Napoletana.

But this mellow mood is quickly broken by a sudden rush of adrenaline.

There's a fight going on in front of the station. Teenage testosterone is pumped to overload as a gang of boys pick on a young black man who's not giving up. It's clear there's an argument over something—a scooter, a girl. Those of us bystanding move back and watch. The mass of volatile youth moves around the street from one side of the station to the other in an angry wave, shouting, ready to explode.

Two girls intervene with the gang leader, pleading to no avail and no sign of police or security either. The black teenager rides away, a girl jumping on behind him. Boys try to pull him off and run after him. More scooters rev up. Shouts ensue. The fight is now on wheels.

My bystander friends and I release a collective outbreath. What happened to the magical, fragrant Sorrento? Italian machismo is what. Teenagers learning the skills of men in this violent society that has bred Machiavelli, the mafia and the mamma's boy.

Things cool down at the station and I sit on the one and only bench to wait for the bus. Slowly, more and more people show up, oblivious of what just happened, to take the last return to Napoli. Couples mostly, the occasional elderly gentleman in a fedora and a flock of young women whose dresses are tighter than tourniquets. This pleasant change from the outburst of *aggressione* makes me marvel at the spectrum of humanity I'm experiencing in one day.

Finally, the bus rolls up and after finding our spots inside, I settle in for the three-hour ride.

Stopping on the outskirts of the city, a group of African migrants climb aboard with folding tables and large bags of unsold wares they've been hawking on the street. The pungent smell of stale sweat pervades the limited air supply on the bus.

Driving through the outer districts of Naples in the dark, I'm working on breathing easy—well actually, just breathing—and not expecting trouble when I arrive.

"*Ultima fermata,*" the driver announces as we stop and everyone gets out. This is not the stop I'm expecting.

"*Dov'è Piazza Garibaldi?*" I ask.

He points ahead and I step out into the night and some cool fresh air. No saunter, no stroll, no relaxed breathing. I have a stride with a purpose. Get to a taxi as fast as possible.

I see a group of parked white cabs up ahead, drivers smoking, chatting, staying awake for the next fare. One of them catches my wave and opens his door for me.

"*Via Francesco Girardi, per favore,*" I tell him as I settle into the comfort of the back seat and we pull away.

€20 later, I climb the ten flights to I Fiori di Napoli, exhausted, safe and immensely satisfied.

Silence of
the Yams

It's my last day here. Manuela has been so kind and informative and runs I Fiori like a mother. I feel safe and cared for and for the few days I'm here, part of her family.

But it's the man whom I met when I first arrived that interests me. Returning from the bathroom, I find him in my room making my bed. He apologizes and leaves quickly. I find him fascinating, so meek and quiet yet his presence pervades the place like a ghost. Can he walk through walls?

I look out the window and see him folding laundry on the balcony below. I can't quite figure him out. He's potentially creepy yet friendly and helpful and has sad eyes.

Manuela must trust him with I Fiori, so I deduce he's okay. But did he do something bad years ago? Did she take him in and give him a second chance? Is he a man with a buried past that's trying to be forgotten? Will he serve me somebody's liver with fava beans and a glass of chianti? Maybe some sweet potatoes on the side?

After a quick breakfast, I head out to the Egg Castle, which sounds like something you'd find in Legoland. In Italian, it's much more romantic: Castel dell'Ovo.

It's a short walk down to the harbor and the heat is on, even at this time of day.

I use Google Maps to get around, but it's still sending me in circles. Maybe the Italian version is designed to give you the true experience of Italy, taking you the wrong way so you discover new places and are forced to talk to people.

I ditch directions and stop for refreshment.

Stepping into a *caffè,* all dark polished wood with a long marble bar, I order my favorite *granita al limone.* The bartender is in uniform, confirming this is a well-to-do establishment, and makes my *granita* to perfection, served in a heavy pedestal glass. I sip and start to cool down. It's at moments like these I'm glad to be sent the wrong way.

After another sip, I realize there is no wrong way.

As I approach the imposing fortifications of Castel dell'Ovo, I observe local life all around me. Bikini-clad women lie on the rocks of the bay like geckos frying in the sun; boys jump from a low wall with loud yells, splashing into the water. Heat clearly dictates behavior around here.

Inside, I walk quickly from shade to shade with nothing really grabbing my attention. Built by the Normans on their conquering path down to Sicily, it's got that functional 12th-century look about it—boxy but safe.

Legend has it there's a magical egg in the foundations, hence the name. If the egg is broken, it means the fall of Naples. I guess it's still there.

The castle may be older than Castel Sant'Elmo, but it lacks the view and the atmosphere and there's way more tourists. I end up leaving sooner than later with the nagging feeling I missed something. Maybe I just wasn't in the mood.

Back on the street I am confronted by a giant blot on the historic landscape that bears the unmistakeable likeness to a cruise ship. This thing is so big it makes Napoli look small. It must be five city-blocks long and dominates the harbor like an ocean-going tourist ghetto, which is exactly what it is.

Why? I ask, not expecting an answer.

I'll tell you why—money. Tourist Euros that Naples needs to survive. A floating city of out-of-towners with a few hours to kill and money to burn, taking trophies back to their friends to show they've 'been' to Naples. No, you've not been to Naples. You don't have a clue what it's like to be here.

The blight of cruise ships has created negative impacts on many historic cities, especially Venice, and not just in Italy. More and more family-run businesses catering for local residents are closing to become tourist shops.

The cruise ships empty their passengers to see the sights and spend their money, leaving a trail of litter behind them putting stress on the local utilities, while the ships keep running in dock, adding to the pollution.

Here in Naples that's a joke. The streets are already overflowing with trash and the pollution is way above legal levels.

The defense for all this is the local economy. But if there's no city left to see, what then? It's a short-term self-centered view, especially in this era of global warming and climate change.

It makes me want to go home, wherever that is.

Rant over, I walk into the Galleria Umberto, the inspiration for the giant glass-and-steel Galleria Vittorio Emanuele in Milan, and browse for some late lunch. There's not much I want here but I find a mouthwatering alternative.

The glass display case of La Sfogliatella Mary is full and they are doing fast business. Giangi insisted I try these and now is the time. People snap up the *sfogliatelle*, small, sweet, dense pastries, like there's no tomorrow. I go for a rum baba and I have to have another one immediately. This is going to develop into a serious addiction and I need more than two. With no one around to stop me, I have to exert some self-control. I envision the consequences of four or five of these things in my stomach and decide I don't want to mop up the floor. I'll savor the memory and come back later.

High on sugar and a touch of rum, I stroll down Via Toledo with a smile on my face. A man with eight dogs is causing a stir on the sidewalk. Big, buff and proud of his canine display, he's surrounded by women who have stopped to talk to him. I get this side of Napoli and its people. Display is of prime importance in Italian society and here, that *bella figura* is a unique mix of rags and riches, of a noble past and a battered present awash with color and noise and life.

Napoli is truly one of a kind and I have fallen in love with it.

The Security Scam

I'm packed and ready to get on a plane. With a sweet goodbye to Manuela, I tell her I'll stay next time I'm in Napoli, even if Hannibal does make dinner.

'See Naples and die,' as the saying went from the Grand Tour, although it sounds more like a threat than an invitation. The accurate meaning extolls the magnificence of the city: 'Once you've seen Naples, you are free to die.'

Even though I've seen Naples in all her battered beauty, I'm not ready to die yet, but the prospect did cross my mind considering where I'm headed.

Out on the street, I pull my lightweight bag down towards the ferry building and the airport bus.

On the way, two men and a woman are having a heated argument. It's not clear why, but car doors are open, arms are waving and there's a lot of pacing back and forth. It's impossible to tell if it's a romantic struggle or a traffic incident. The two tend to be intertwined in Italy.

At the ferry, finding the stop for the Alibus is not as easy as I'd hoped. I'm looking at Google Maps but it doesn't show the roadworks that mess things up. This looks like where I'm supposed to be. I ask an older couple sitting on a bench but the woman recoils like I'm going to rob her as her husband glares at me.

Do I look that mean? No, but this is a clear reflection of street life in Naples.

I stand in the shade and wait. Across the street, a line begins to form of people and suitcases. I make my way over and see the sign: Alibus. Sure enough, along comes my ride to the airport.

The bus seats are hard, uncomfortable, dirty and broken.

Dear Italy, I know it's more important to hide billions in corruption accounts and line the pockets of politicians. I know *la moda* is more important than an efficient infrastructure. I know that fresh pasta is more important than punctuality. But please, can you fix my seat?

Inside the airport is a different matter. It's clean and there's a decent lunch waiting for me at one of the eateries followed by strong *caffè*.

Replete and ready for travel, I check in and head for security. So far in all my flying around Europe, I've had an easy time of it, just not today—I've packed my precious Davine's Oil Non Oil in my carry-on and it's over the allowance.

The pretty young security guard examines the contents of my bag on her X-ray screen and says to her pretty young colleague to open my bag. She asks me to take out my hair product and informs me I can't take it on the plane.

I tell her it cost me €18 and would she like to buy it from me? Her brief smile is followed by a stare.

Reluctantly, I give it to her and zip up my bag.

The other side of security, we are made to walk through the pornographic duty-free section on our way to the gate. In front of me is an aisle of beauty products. Hair products. Davine's Oil Non Oil is €25 for a bottle half the size of my confiscated container.

Now I'm fuming. The whole thing is a scam! This is nothing about terrorism—this is commerce. They took my stuff and now they're trying to sell it back to me at a profit.

I walk past all this extortion trying not to cause a scene, although that would be perfectly acceptable. At some point I'll laugh at this. The sheer absurdity of air travel security and the scams that have gone on since 9/11 in the name of global safety are an excuse for something else entirely.

How did we let this happen?

Arriving at the gate, I see a prominent sign in Italian followed by its English translation: It Is Not Allowed To Touch Genitalia At Any Time.

Now I'm laughing.

For those perplexed by this sign, a footnote: Italian men, most likely from the south, have a habit of scratching their balls in public as a sign of virility.

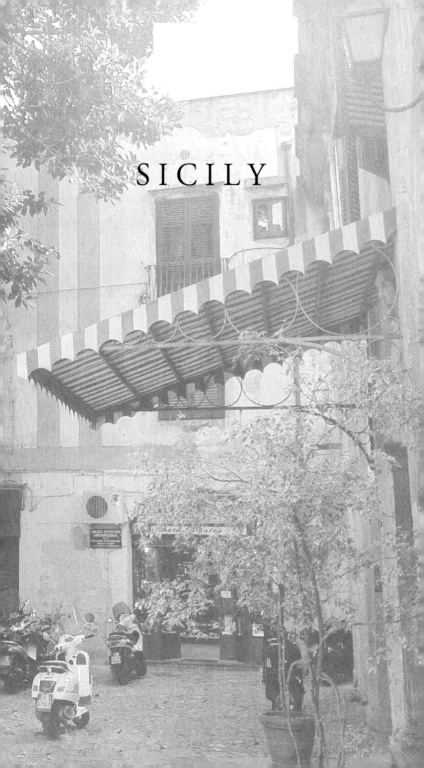

SICILY

Landing
in Palermo

Touching down in Punta Raisi airport, I have the feeling I'm in for more of an adventure than I bargained for. I'm in Sicily where the food is simple, the people are warm and the weather is hot. It's also the home of the Cosa Nostra so I'm a little on edge about what to expect on a dark night, even though I've just spent a few of them in Naples. But given I'm a trusting soul and six foot five, I'm pretty confident that nothing too bad is going to happen as the average height of a Sicilian is five foot six, not that that makes much of a difference.

I walk out of the small airport to the taxi stand. There's not much going on. A large man sits in a captain's chair taking taxi orders and giving them to the drivers who stand around waiting, smoking. The plane wasn't full so he's got maybe three or four fares. I'm not one of them.

I've booked an apartment in downtown Palermo and

instructed to wait for Alberto, who'll be picking me up.

It's hot. Hotter than Napoli. Hotter than expected. I'm in the Mezzogiorno, the name given to the southern regions of Italy for the heat and brightness of the midday sun.

I lean against a wall in the shade and watch. Finally a short man walks toward me.

"Navyo?"

"*Sì. Alberto?*"

His English is very good, surprising so far south. He congratulates me for arriving in one piece as Punta Raisi, he tells me, is the most dangerous airport in Italy and one of the most dangerous in the world.

That's reassuring.

I walk with him, assuming we're headed to his car, which we are in a round about sort of way. Instead of going to the parking lot, we step over a barrier and walk across a dry arid area, cross an onramp, over another barrier, more parched land and onto a frontage road.

I feel like I'm in another movie. Not a Sophia Loren romance but a gritty Pasolini drama with wide shots of hot dry nothing, dust from a car in the distance. A tight shot on my eyes. Sweat on my brow. Worrying.

Alberto snaps me out of it with a cheery wave.

"Here's my summer house," he proclaims proudly.

We step through the gate of a trailer park and there is his car. So this is how they drive in Sicily. Must be a petrol saving strategy—walk half way and then get in. Except we're not getting in.

A slender long-haired olive-skinned beauty in a sarong approaches me with a huge smile.

"Navyo!"

I love that people I've never met know me by name. It gives me a sense of celebrity.

Caterina, my host, introduces herself and lets me know it's going to be a while before we leave for the apartment. Are we going to walk, I wonder? She suggests I go for a dip and that is something I am not going to refuse.

I change my clothes in a trailer and step back out. Alberto introduces me to his wife, who does not smile, and their son who must be about three, kicking a ball. Donning flip flops, I head to the water. The rocks look razor sharp and continue down into the sea. I'm supposed to swim in this? Alberto motions to me to push myself off into deeper water and then heads back to the house

Not being the strongest swimmer, I decide to paddle a bit and float in the shallows. The water is warm and this is the first time, however brief, I am in the Mediterranean, technically the Thyrrenian. Further down, some teenage boys in swimming trunks try to throw each other into the sea. Extras from the Pasolini shoot, I imagine.

I'm alone in the Med with razor rocks and Pasolini's extras and I've left my phone, my wallet and my clothes in a trailer with people I don't know in Sicily. Am I stupid?

No, I'm trusting.

I relax into the moment and feel the warmth of the

water caress my body in its swells, the sound of the boys in the distance. A jet roars overhead to land, wheels down, flaps up, reminding me how close we are to the airport. A short walk, in fact.

I clamber carefully out trying not to lacerate myself, find my flip flops and towel and return to the trailer, my belongings where I left them.

Before long, everyone's ready to go. This time we're actually getting into a car. It's a tight squeeze, but we manage. This is one of those 'How many people can you fit in a Fiat' moments, even though there's only five of us, plus luggage. With my long legs, I'm lucky I'm in the front, albeit with a large bag on my lap.

The sun is getting low, its rich golden light amplified by the heat and haze as we drive along the coast, windows down, elbows out, the warm evening wind blowing into the car. This is a perfect time for Pasolini to shoot, but as he's been dead for decades it's going to have to be inside my head.

On the highway, Alberto asks me if I've heard of Giovanni Falcone. The name rings a bell. I remember black-and-white photos of bombed-out cars and carnage.

"Falcone was the local magistrate prosecuting the mafia in the '80s and '90s, from local bosses all the way to the top. It was right here on the highway on the 23rd of May 1992 that he and his wife were killed on their way from the airport when the road exploded."

Alberto points uphill. I can just make out the words

'NO MAFIA' painted on a white pillar.

"That's where they pressed the detonator."

My reassurance disappears completely.

We drive past a mountainous outcrop.

"Remember when I said the airport was dangerous?"

How could I forget.

"This was the site of an infamous plane disaster."

I'm not sure I can take any more and I've only just got here. I'm also not sure accidents actually happen in Sicily. They seem far too convenient.

Pulling off the highway in one piece, we turn into a grove of tall palm trees and park in the lot of a restaurant.

Most of the outdoor tables are empty and we choose the perfect spot. Sitting down together it's nice to finally connect. Alberto's wife even gives me a cursory smile before returning to her concerned frown. Is there something she's not telling me—or can't tell me?

Sharing delicious pizza with new friends under the palms on a warm Sicilian evening filled with the fragrance of jasmine, thoughts of dangerous airports and exploding highways drift away and I'm again under the spell of Italy. A deep well of gratitude rises up in me and I feel content in a way only this can provide.

Until it's time to pay.

We split up the tab and I give Alberto a €20 bill. He goes into the restaurant and returns empty handed.

"Sorry, they don't have change. I'll get it to you later."

Only that later will never come and after tonight I will

never see him or my change again. It's then I remember I'm dealing with a Sicilian and I'm just an American tourist which means money. In this unspoken transaction, I write it off as a cab fare.

Captive at night driving into the city, I decide to go with the flow. Besides, I'm too exhausted to put up a fight.

In the center of Palermo, we stop in a small dimly-lit piazza tucked behind a main street. Caterina and I get out with my luggage and Alberto and family drive off into the night.

"Mind your head," she warns as we go through a very old door about five feet high and climb some very old stairs.

After a quick tour of the apartment, Caterina takes off. As for me, I can't stay awake a moment longer.

Faded
Glory

A cold shower freshens me up from my first solid night's sleep in a while. The apartment is absolutely beautiful and I've got it to myself for the next few days as Caterina is staying with a friend. It has all the hallmarks of creativity, hippie elegance and a woman's touch. If I lived here I wouldn't change it much. It's just my style.

Morning sunlight streams in through gauze curtains casting a bright glaze over the polished hardwood floor. I step in the kitchen and boil some water in a small pan. Italians are not known for their kettles.

Sitting in the quiet tranquil space of the living room sipping green tea, I feel myself drop into really being here, in the apartment, in Palermo, in Sicily.

I lead a very privileged life, something I do not forget for a moment. I also have to acknowledge that I created this. It's not as if it just happened by sheer luck. I put my time, my focus, my deliberate intent and purpose into traveling here. I did all I could and worked with the energy behind it, seeing my wishes come about in my mind's eye.

I just knew I was going.

That acknowledgment helps me immensely in my transition from being the lost little boy missing his dead mother to the world traveler living the life of his dreams.

My journey into the deeper layers of manhood can only happen by taking risks and jumping into life. Looking back, it seems my mother's death was the push I needed. Coming to Sicily feels the biggest jump I've taken in a long time.

Geographically, Palermo is closer to North Africa than Naples. From what I've read, it's a unique place with a unique history of cultural influences I can't wait to explore.

Heading out through the small wooden door and along a narrow alleyway, I come to the main street. I'm close to Quattro Canti, Four Corners, a central intersection where two main streets of Palermo form a cross. It's busy, noisy and polluted, much more than Naples. Palermo is, in fact, the most polluted city in Italy. Thank you, fossil fuels.

The sidewalks are small and it's a tight squeeze negotiating real estate. I need space.

Cutting through a small side street, I come into a deserted piazza with a monumental circular fountain populated by statues of naked people, Fontana Pretoria. It's huge, something you'd expect in Rome. Here it feels tucked away out of sight. You'd really have to know about it or stumble on it like I've just done. But then I'm all for that.

Mythological figures and Olympic heroes stand about like it was yesterday. Originally built in Florence, it was designed for the gardens of a villa. Many of the statues were damaged or lost in transit, which means this is just part of an even grander creation.

I linger in the beauty of this hidden gem, a welcome break from noise and fumes. Only later will I learn this was dubbed the Piazza of Shame for the corrupt politicians of the city as these nude figures are in front of the town hall.

Why am I not surprised?

Out on the main street, I'm thrust back into modern life.

Through an archway, I peek into an open courtyard, white walls and sand-yellow window frames vibrant in the natural light; a Vespa stands parked at the base of a tall palm tree occupying the central space, reaching all the way up to the third floor before its fronds open.

Across a main street in a small piazza stands another tall palm tree in front of the Baroque facade of a church, the architectural mark of the Spanish from their six centuries of occupation.

The combination of direct Mediterranean light, Islamic and Baroque architecture, palm trees and small prickly-pear cactus give Palermo a distinctive look unlike anywhere else in Italy. But then this is not really Italy.

Even though I've just got here, it seems another country. They don't even call Italy the mainland, but *il continente,* the continent.

Teatro Massimo is the largest opera house in Italy, a stature that affirms not just Sicilians love for opera but for producing singers. In its shadow, across Piazza Verdi, is Bar Ruvolo which I've been told serves the best coffee in Palermo.

Sitting in the shade of a large tree overlooking the Teatro, I order *caffè e pasticcino*, a Sicilian creme-filled pastry.

The espresso is strong, stronger than Neapolitan coffee, which is already strong. Not bitter from over-roasting like the undrinkable American tar, it's a smooth powerful lift that doesn't stop. An espresso in Palermo, I've read, is 'a superconcentration of all the caffeine in the world.'

In typical Sicilian style there's a lot of hanging about. A large dog is collapsed in the sun and I take this as a sign. Do nothing. Wait until it cools down, then get up.

If I follow his example, I won't see much of Palermo. A traditional popular song blares from one of the blue-and-white tourist rickshaws, its distorted volume my cue to leave.

Wandering off the main streets, I'm struck by the poverty here. Poorer than Naples, it still retains the faded glory that defines the island.

The architecture is a mix of influences from classical

Greek and Roman to the elegant patterns and curves of the Arabs, from austere Norman stonework to the decorative Spanish Baroque. This is a culture clash of a place that has absorbed the influence of its conquerors and made it its own.

Sicily is a melting pot, stewing for millennia. The food, the architecture, the DNA, it's all from elsewhere. These assimilations are what makes the island and its people so unique. Throw in an active volcano, Mount Etna, and you've got a living, breathing island.

Amidst all this history is a modern city with traffic and commerce. Even so, there's an overwhelming sense of decay, and yet somehow its people have continued to thrive as it slowly crumbles. There are the ever-present statues of the human form, but they've gathered years of dirt and grime that even the rain can't wash away.

Behind the main streets, that decay becomes more obvious. The roads are unpaved, the buildings are in seriously bad shape, but it's got character. Tourists flock to experience this character which means profit. Why mess that up with expensive repairs?

I begin to understand the meanings behind Sicilian life: Don't disturb our history. Leave us alone. And we're not Italian. Just come here and spend your money. Enjoy our faded glory, how we've survived three thousand years of foreign rule. And when you leave, take a romantic memory with you of a world apart, a timeless place of wonderful food and beautiful women, of people living on the edge of violence. Remember this place as a scene from the heights of Italian cinema. Don't fuck with us and we might not fuck with you. Now sit down and enjoy your *caffè*.

According to my city guide, Don Saro is supposed to show up at the Quattro Canti intersection around eleven o'clock to give a free tour of the city. I head back to whence I came, look for his green umbrella and wait. Fifteen minutes, thirty minutes. No umbrella, no Don Saro, no tour, just lots of pestering by horse-and-buggy drivers wanting me to pay through the nose for their tour of the town.

In search of shade, I enter the theatrical interior of Santissimo Salvatore. Unlike any church I've seen before, its chairs, instead of pews, are arranged in a semicircle facing a stage on which stands the pulpit, as if the priest is going to put on a show—which, in a way, he is. He will certainly be in costume and it's not as if he hasn't rehearsed his lines. A throne sits on a raised dais in front of tall candles, while a balcony to one side overlooks the audience. The entire stage is made for a production.

Palermo and no doubt all of Sicily is a stage set, its inhabitants in costume playing roles honed for centuries.

Back on the streets, I hike up towards the Duomo.

The grounds are filling with tourists and high school kids, who in this moment decide to have a water fight. What fun, except I'd rather avoid a drenching even though it might cool me down. I skirt around the fray to the entrance.

From the outside, the cathedral looks a magnificent sandstone work of art, much different to when it was built. Since then, it has been converted into a mosque, back into a church and had significant additions and alterations along the way.

Inside, it's less magnificent. The exterior advertises something the interior just does not deliver. It's a standard Roman Catholic church without elegance or style that has erased its history. I feel cheated and disappointed.

Then I notice something. Just as in Rome in Michelangelo's Santa Maria degli Angeli e Martiri, a brass meridian lies diagonally across the cathedral floor with signs of the zodiac on either side. Again, such pagan symbols still seem out of place in a Catholic church, but this is an astronomical device to calculate Easter—the first Sunday after the first full moon after the Spring Equinox, a moveable date that the church needs to reliably predict. Missing the Resurrection by a day or two would not be good. It could cause liturgical havoc.

On my way out, something grabs my attention that I would never imagine in a Catholic church, far less tolerable than pagan symbols—on one of the columns of the entrance is carved a page from the Quran.

In America, this would have been removed long ago. But thankfully, this is not America, this is Sicily where everyone comes from somewhere else.

Pause for thought.

Sicily has something to teach the religious right and culturally fixed, not just in America, but the world. Even its boot-shaped neighbor, *il continente*—tolerance, acceptance, assimilation, evolution.

During its two centuries of Arab rule—when the cathedral was a mosque—Sicily was more scientifically advanced, educated and developed than Continental Europe. Literacy was much higher than the centuries of Christianity that followed. By the early 20th century, Sicilian literacy was at its lowest point, while religious intolerance was firmly back in the Catholic saddle.

It appears keeping people uneducated has some religious benefits.

Outside sits a colorful antidote to all this seriousness— a rainbow-colored boat on wheels with large rocks inside and flowers decorating the hull. Something you'd find at Burning Man.

This is the float for an effigy of Santa Rosalia, one of the patron saints of Palermo who miraculously 'cured' a nasty bout of the plague in the 17th century. Every year, she's paraded through the city to ensure its protection. Customs die hard here. Come to think of it, they don't die at all.

After a nap at the apartment, I head back out again. As I go down the stone stairs, I'm met with an odor I can't place and I'd rather not place. It smells like boiling dead something. Festering. Rank. Putrid. Has there been a sacrifice? Is this a Sicilian custom? Does it include tourists?

I descend past an open door where the odor is its most pungent. Whatever is being cooked in there has been dug up from a grave. I want to heave. The sound of African music accompanies the odor as I hurry to the front door.

Out in the fresh air, I take some deep breaths to exhume the dead from my lungs. What the hell *was* that?

No, I still don't want to know.

Spinnato's is supposed to be the place for pastries and coffee. So was Bar Ruvolo. I'm getting the hang of this—there is more than one place that is the best in Italy.

Antico Caffè Spinnato has been in business since 1860 and retains that old-world charm with a well-kept dark wood interior and large polished tables. The regular clientele dress up to come here, unlike the tourists. Even though I try to blend in, it's obvious I'm not from around here. But dressing up is all part of *bella figura*, that uniquely Italian concept that stretches beyond mere style.

The pastry counter is almost as long as the bar, but I'm not in the mood. I order a *granita,* another Arab import, with a shot of coffee mixed in to beat the heat and give me a lift at the same time. That lift, stronger than expected, pushes me back outside for more exploration, with one noisy unbreathable problem—it's rush hour.

Full buses angrily pump out fumes as I hold my breath and try and cross the street, avoiding cars and buzzing *motorini* weaving their way through every available space. This is mayhem.

Arriving on the other side in one piece, I get my bearings.

Looking remarkably similar to Teatro Massimo, although a little smaller, Teatro Politeama sits back in its own piazza away from traffic.

A grand triumphal arch presents the front of the circular building. Flying from the top, bronze horses rear up either side of a rider on his chariot, representing the triumph of the Olympic Games. It's yet another reminder of the Greeks who first settled here almost three thousand years ago.

Teatro Politeama holds the same sense of grandeur, culture and music that Sicily is famous for and deeply proud of. The theater is home to the Orchestra Sinfonica Siciliana, its concert season displayed outside.

Back up the busy main street, I'm confronted by more commerce. But this big shopping area has one thing going for it: Piazza Castelnuovo, a sprawling space landscaped with palm trees, too many to count.

I rest a moment in their shade and contemplate this paradox of Palermo—the modern city and the money to keep it running, the commerce and big-name retail stores, and yet so much of this facade hides its crumbling neighborhoods. With Italy's forty-five percent income tax, you'd expect something more. Is it really just about food and clothes and *la dolce vita?*

All the locals I've spoken with in every town I've visited tell the same story—frustration and anger at corrupt politicians who live the high life off taxpayers' money while the people of Italy suffer a broken system.

The further south, the more poverty. Here in Sicilia, it's in a class of its own. Politicians in Rome and Milan have referred to the Mezzogiorno as 'the problem of the south' for decades—a problem for which there is no solution. Tradition, corruption and rural justice have very deep roots on the island.

It's impossible to write about Palermo and not mention the mafia.

It wasn't until the 1960s that its existence was even publicly acknowledged. Previously, such venerated authorities as the Oxford English Dictionary defined it in vague terms, while the Italian government, mainstream media and the Vatican denied its existence altogether.

It doesn't take a genius to figure this out—mafia corruption extended into every level of society and still does.

Palermo is famously home to the mafia, who took control of the city governance for decades. Their visible legacy from that time is one that goes beyond shame, so I doubt if the nudes of Fontana Pretoria facing city hall are enough of a statement. They decimated the historic heart of the city in what is known as the Sack of Palermo.

During the 1950s and '60s, the mafia-controlled city orchestrated the destruction of beautiful parks, palaces and other elegant buildings to build concrete apartment blocks made of shoddy materials in their place. This was expanded in the outskirts of the city to house the poorer folks displaced from the center with buildings even worse.

All this construction was approved to launder drug money.

This cultural atrocity is hard to fathom. Why would a people so proud of their heritage destroy it to hide their ill-gotten gains? One can only assume it is the deepest point in Dante's depiction of purgatory: greed.

The more I think about it, the more I want to stay in the apartment all day. But that's not why I came here. That's not why anyone comes here. If Sicily was fixed up, tourism would die.

Italy, especially Sicilia, is about atmosphere.

The Triumph
of Death

The next morning I wake up feeling down and in need of a lift. I decide to head for the harbor. Maybe some sea air will change my mood and give me some context.

Crossing the main harbor road, I come to the somewhat parched empty space of Parco Foro Italico, the sea in the distance ahead of me. Palm trees dot the perimeter of the park, a protection between the sea and the city walls. It's getting hot out here and it's still early. By the time I get to the waterfront, I'm having to slow down. Colorful square benches looking arty but uncomfortable line the promenade.

To the left, docks and cranes stand in miniature at the base of the huge rock dominating the skyline, Monte Pellegrino. To the right, rowboats sit moored in an inlet, the water so clear it looks as if they're suspended in mid air. Behind them in the distance, rows of apartment blocks ruin the view, a sad reminder of the Sack of Palermo.

I'm at some invisible nexus, an arid no-man's land protecting me from urban life.

A warm sea breeze clears my mind and cleans my soul, bringing fresh life to my weary bones. I turn around to see the city spread out before me as an arriving trader may have done centuries ago, an opportunity, an adventure.

Back over the dry empty space, I re-enter the city through Porta dei Greci, the Gate of the Greeks.

The Greeks were the first foreign settlers on the island. For centuries, Greek was the language spoken in Sicily, which accounts for why it was called Magna Grecia, Greater Greece. The Romans even referred to Sicilians as Greeks.

Such are the rich layers of history here, even though I entered through the Greek Gate, I'm in the old Arab Quarter, La Kalsa, at one time the city center.

The Arabs were a tolerant lot and allowed a live-and-let-live society. Their legacy is everywhere from dried pasta to irrigation, almonds, oranges, lemons, pistachios and sugar cane, which eventually became the *dolci* Sicily is famous for—cassata, cannoli and gelato. As much as Florentines would like to think they invented gelato, it was Sicily, thanks to the Arabs, that takes the prize.

Much of what we now take for granted is owed to the Arabs who brought paper money, compass navigation and their numeric system we still use today to Sicily and thus to Europe and the Americas. Food for thought considering the state of the world.

Leaving La Kalsa, I find more of the city crumbling yet no one seems to care. The remains of a bombed-out building stand in a back street, fallen walls and rubble untouched since World War Two. Then I suddenly remember—character, atmosphere, Pasolini.

Rounding a corner, I approach another church. The main entrance is open and it looks like a wedding is underway. I've seen this before in Rome and it's been okay to step inside. Just not this time. The door of a black Maserati Quattroporte opens and a man in a sharp blue suit and sunglasses steps out and turns toward me, his palm outstretched. I give a friendly wave and move on. He does not smile.

Giant banyan fig trees with long hanging branches and large exposed roots occupy the central garden of a small piazza. However magnificent they may be, they survive by strangling their hosts, smaller trees within their suffocating embrace.

The imposing walls of a large *palazzo* loom over the garden, giving an unsettling air of both beauty and dread, something definitively Sicilian.

Next to the garden is a restaurant, Al Covo dei Beati Paoli, The Cave of the Blessed Pauls. The emblem of the restaurant is a dark hooded figure that looks intent on malice. Is he a waiter?

I'm not so sure about this place or the *palazzo* or the trees. But hunger trumps hunches and I find a seat at an outdoor table close to the sidewalk, just in case. A waiter comes over and takes my order without so much of a *buongiorno* or a smile.

While I wait, I look up the restaurant on my iPhone.

The Beati Paoli were a secret sect that met in the vaults and underground passages of Palermo by candlelight wearing black hooded robes for anonymity. Each were given names and titles like a brotherhood, avengers administering private justice and executions for family vendettas. They were the precursors of the mafia.

Do I really want to eat here?

With no lunch in sight, I continue reading about the *palazzo* across the way.

Palazzo Chiaramonte Steri is the old headquarters of the Spanish Inquisition.

This is not a happy place.

For three hundred years, their inhuman, barbaric cruelty had but one aim in mind—to eradicate any trace of foreign thinking or behavior and establish strict Catholicism as the dominant religion.

Ironically, Palazzo Chiaramonte Steri was originally built by the Arabs to make their brilliantly colored *maiolica* pottery, still evident all over Sicily. How can a place intended for such simple beauty become host to such torture and pain?

Gone was the multi-faith, multilingual tolerance of the Arabs and Normans. During the Inquisition, Jews, Muslims, Orthodox Greeks and questionable Christians were thrown into the fetid underground warehouse with no toilet or place to lie down. Many would spend months or even years there before facing trial, if they survived. The lucky few who had money could buy themselves out. So much for a moral crusade.

The grim waiter finally returns with my order. Is it poisoned?

While I carefully tuck into a rather dull, mediocre pizza, a barefoot young waif about ten years old in a torn and dirty dress comes up to my table on the street side of the low iron fence.

"*Signore, signore,*" she pleads, her little hand outstretched, the lack of hope in her dark eyes.

I could have given her some change or some food, but instead I wave her off.

Why did I do that? Am I possessed by the Beati Paoli?

She probably has to give the money to some nefarious adult who keeps it for himself. Still, my conscience took a dent. I abandon my half-finished pizza, pay the bill and leave.

Feeling guilty yet undeterred by the harsh reality of Sicilian street life, I make my way to the Galleria Regionale just around the corner, as recommended by my Florentine host Judith, where there is a must-see fresco. That should brighten me up.

On my arrival, I am unwelcomed by an unfriendly old man at a battered old wooden desk. Do they actually want visitors? I buy my ticket and *thud!*, he inks it with his rubber stamp and pushes it towards me without a look or a nod. How long can the poor desk stand his beating? But I take this as a metaphor of life in Sicily.

I pick up my bruised ticket and go in.

The main exhibit is the Triumph of Death, an anonymous fresco from the 15th century lit up in its own gallery.

In the top section of this giant work, a man walks his dogs, another plays the harp, others gather round a fountain as if nothing is happening. In the center, Death is riding a large dead horse over dead priests surrounded by dead people. Designed to be scary. Designed to make you go to church.

Now the man at the desk makes sense.

But there's something more to this fresco, something modern, something abstract. The half-decaying horse reminds me of Picasso's brutal Guernica. It transcends time, just like death. And just like death, it feels appropriate for brutal Palermo.

I wander into another room and start taking photos. A woman with a badge starts yelling at me in Italian. Okay, okay, I'll stop. There are staff in every room waiting to do this to more unsuspecting visitors. The majority of artifacts on display are of the Madonna and Child, that ever-present icon of the nurturing feminine, a singularly sweet concept that doesn't quite translate here. There's an overwhelmingly dark feeling about the place.

Is everyone really having a bad day? Or has the

Triumph of Death come to life?

I have to get out of here.

Palermo on the outside can seem dangerous, the dirt and noise and survival on the street, the big fashion shops busting with life and color while the bakeries serve stale bread. I've eaten almost nothing fresh since I came here. And from noon to four everything is closed. People stand around in the shade looking dodgy. The whole place is dodgy.

After centuries of being conquered by foreigners, of torture by the Inquisition, of the Beati Paoli, of feudal family vendettas, of mafia intimidation, violence is part of Sicilian life. It's in their blood.

There's something much older here, older than Naples or Rome, something deep, dark and brooding, just like its volcano. Not to be messed with.

Like a breath of fresh air, Judith texts me she arrived in Palermo yesterday and can meet this afternoon if I'm available.

We convene in Piazza Bellini, not far from the apartment. I can't believe we're here at the same time. It seems fate drew us together for reasons yet to be revealed.

She used to live here and was a tour guide, so she's highly knowledgeable.

To demonstrate that knowledge, she directs my attention across the piazza to the three red Islamic domes of the church of San Cataldo, yet more cultural infusion. But the main event is next door.

La Martorana is a church named after a pastry, Judith informs me, as the nuns who lived at the attached convent were known for their delicious almond delicacies. It seems somehow fitting that sugar and religion be combined in this way, especially in Sicily.

Here is that rich blend of Norman, Byzantine and Baroque architecture. But it doesn't reveal its contents from the outside—simple, unrefined Norman stonework with a decorative Baroque facade slapped on the front by the Spanish.

Inside, it's another matter.

Shafts of glorious sunlight emblazon colorful frescos; high arches and the entire ceiling are covered in shimmering gold-tile mosaics. Everything is gleaming and magical. This is the exquisite drama I've been looking for.

Judith tells me of Norman King Roger II, the first King of Sicily, who built this place and is depicted in gold being crowned by none other than Christ himself. What a guy. Must have been a big thinker.

As the Normans took over from the Arabs, Roger was fluent in Arabic, Greek, French and Latin and dressed in Arab clothes to court. During his reign, Sicily was a multi-faith, multilingual place that was the example for all to follow.

If only that succeeded.

I'm transfixed by Judith's wealth of knowledge and wish I had her inside my head while I've been visiting the rest of Palermo.

She tells me of the Palatine Chapel and the cathedral at Monreale, not too far from Palermo, even greater examples of multi-racial artisans and gold mosaics, giving me more reasons to return.

After all this education, we wind up at a bar for *granita,* this time with traditional sweet brioche, an odd combination which stops you getting freeze-mouth. I can't wait to try it on my friends.

My host Caterina joins us as arranged and we have a genuine Couchsurfing meetup. Three diverse people—a Florentine American, a Californian Brit and a Sicilian, all connecting over *granita al limone con brioche* in Palermo. It's moments like these that make it all worthwhile.

Accordions
in the Sunset

Today I stay at home to sleep off a bad stomach and worse headache. Maybe the pizza was poisoned yesterday.

As I lie in bed feeling sorry for myself, unable to explore Palermo, I realize this is from nothing I've eaten. This is another wave of processing the loss of my mother. Just when I thought I'd immersed myself in foreign lands, new friends and the thrill of adventure, here it is. It's not something I can avoid. It's my own Triumph of Death.

Caterina stops by and makes me a pot of chamomile tea. I feel her caring filling the maternal void, something that does not go unnoticed. It may be a small thing, but its effects are tremendously healing.

After more sleep, slowly, painstakingly, I return to some semblance of normal, if there is such a thing. By about six, I'm ready to go out.

Taking a gentle stroll to the seafront, I end up at the

marina, the sound of water lapping on boats so peaceful, so calming. And then I hear them.

Faint at first but getting louder as I approach, two men and two women sit on a low wall forming a quartet of accordions. This is not traditional Sicilian music but something more modern, more sweet and soothing, more ambient.

Watching them perform, I have no desire to take photos or record them. This is not to be captured but experienced. As I sit on a grassy knoll behind them, their harmonious sounds provide the soundtrack to the Sicilian sunset. It's one of those moments that can only be found by stepping out into life and being open to discover.

I relax into the music, the fading light, the sea air. Nothing else exists. I'm suspended in time, floating with boats and accordions.

Maybe I should eat something.

Wandering slowly back into the city, I find myself at the small piazza with the strangling banyan trees. Oh no.

Heading to where I think I should be, I'm getting lost. Two women turn into a side street. Maybe I should follow them. Women lead the way, right? Except it's a dead end and they give me some shifty looks as they get into their car.

Now I really am lost. In Palermo. In the dark.

Some loud young men start a fight a few blocks up and I hurriedly turn back towards the Inquisition and the men with hoods. The sense of dread descends in my belly as the metallic taste of fear rises in my mouth. My heart thumps inside my chest.

Accordions. Sunset. Boats. It's all going to be okay.

I quicken my pace toward some lights ahead. Via Vittorio Emanuele, the main street. My savior.

With some long deep breaths, I hike safely home, lock the door and crawl into bed, the memory of accordions lulling me into sleep.

Three Men
and a Boat

Sitting at the table in this beautiful apartment contemplating the day ahead, I hear a knock followed by the key in the front door. Caterina's smile, her natural radiance and physical beauty are not just a welcome sight, but an immediate reminder of feminine grace and power.

She asks me if I want to visit a friend who docked in the marina last night. I'm not about to refuse and we take the fifteen-minute walk together on this hot Sicilian morning.

Gone are the sweet strains of accordions at the marina, just the sound of traffic racing along the busy harbor road.

Arriving at the slip, we are greeted by three burly boatmen, their sun-drenched skin leathered from life at sea.

One is working on a broken radio and looks up to acknowledge us with a big friendly smile.

A tall handsome man with piercing blue eyes is clearly

241

the captain. He climbs over some rigging to give Caterina a hug and I am introduced with a warm, firm handshake.

An older man in a white cap repairs some electrics and asks if I want to help. I twist cables and tie ends to terminals. It's simple stuff, but it feels good to participate.

They're constantly joking in a mix of English and Italian interjected with bursts of laughter, a refreshing change from the dark shadows of the last two days.

Caterina and I go below decks with the captain and coffee is made. He struggles a little with English so she helps translate. They've been at sea for a few weeks, docking in Palermo where all three of them live.

Who would have thought I'd be on a boat with some locals in Sicily? But this is the magic of Couchsurfing.

Up on deck the electrics are online and it's time to go. With more firm handshakes and weatherbeaten smiles, we leave this maritime moment, teeter-tottering on a gangplank over to dry land.

I've met some more Sicilians, I've helped a boat get back to sea and it's not even lunchtime.

By the time we get to Antica Focacceria San Francesco, I'm ready to eat. But this isn't any old sandwich shop, this is the place that changed history and stood up to the mafia.

In 2005, the owner, Vincenzo Ponticello, refused to pay the *pizzo*, the mafia protection money. The restaurant was vandalized and he found death threats. They killed his cat, then his dog. They broke into his car and left the doors open. To this day, he lives under twenty-four-hour police protection.

AddioPizzo was founded a few years later for business owners who refuse to pay the *pizzo,* openly displaying a sticker in their window or the logo on their website. This seems a dangerous proposition considering what happened to Vincenzo, but there is strength in numbers—currently over one thousand businesses are registered with AddioPizzo.

Sitting at a wrought-iron tiled table, we munch on soft and delicious focaccia *panini* filled with tender *prosciutto crudo,* unafraid of the mafia even though they're probably lurking outside or even eating across the room.

On our way up to the apartment, the stench of boiling corpses turns my stomach. The Africans are cooking again with the door open. I still don't know what it is, but I never want to smell this again.

Upstairs, we close the door quickly and make some herbal tea. Caterina is leaving soon for Germany to visit her boyfriend. She's an incredibly lucky woman living the dream of an artist in the flow of life. I envy her until I realize I'm doing the same thing.

I pack my bags and once again, I don't want to leave. There's so much I haven't seen or been able to fully appreciate in this historic layer cake of a city, not to mention the rest of this astonishing island.

After mutual *arrivederci* and *buon viaggi,* it's time for

me to head to the airport and back to Rome. This time, I'm not walking.

Under the Stars

Easyjet have been my airline of choice in Europe and I've had continued good experience with them. Great job. No complaints. I always get an exit-aisle seat as it comes with Speedy Boarding and minimal waiting.

Here in Punta Raisi, the mass of people trying to board is at a complete standstill. The fast lane is not a lane. There isn't a lane, there's just a pile of everyone trying to get to the gate. Squeezed through this chaos, I present my documents to an elegant uniformed man in his sixties who methodically checks our boarding passes with a calm authority, and in a deep baritone welcomes each of us to the flight and bids us a *buon viaggio*. Once we're through, we're rubbing shoulders in the umbilical corridor for another thirty minutes. It takes over an hour to board the plane and it's not even half full.

But what's an hour for a Sicilian? It's only time, and

time is measured by experience. That's sixty minutes of pushing and shoving, talking, laughing, shouting, arguing, waiting and standing around.

If I'm really going to live like an Italian, I need to learn to loiter.

Sitting in the plane as we wait for takeoff, I contemplate why I came here.

It may have been to immerse myself in Sicilian life, to learn more about the people and their history, but the real reason is something deeper. The integration of cultures I've experienced in the last few days is a metaphor of integrating myself—the lost and helpless son grieving his dead mother; the man seeking his innermost identity; the world traveler on his Grand Tour; the writer; the trusting soul living with faith in the invisible. They don't have to be at odds, I don't have to choose one over another. They can all exist together in this one crazy life, this play of form, this dance, this opportunity.

Landing at Fiumicino Airport, I take the Leonardo Express to Termini Station.

Pulling the lightweight green bag down Via Cavour— still such a joy after the weight of the Beast—I see Alessia with her bicycle outside the front door. Perfect timing once again.

She gives me not only a sweet welcome but a sweet surprise. Even though it's not until next week, she's throwing me a birthday dinner party on the roof.

Around nine o'clock, folks start to gather. Vicky is here, Liza from New York, Alessia's friend Matteo and his girlfriend, and Alessia's daughter Ari. The delicious dishes are all vegetarian that she created using local recouped produce. Plus, she's made *tiramisù* from her grandmother's recipe. What more could I want?

With full bellies, we sit and chat under the stars into the wee hours.

I'm feeling so loved, so cared for on my last night in Rome, in Italy, for a while. My journey has been filled with adventure, friends old and new and experiences that could not be bought with money.

Italy in its lingering beauty, the centuries of humanity in its passion play, its art and food and sensual chaos, its light and landscape, has been not just my context but the very inspiration to live. Its ever-present expressions of the feminine in all her forms have nourished me in a way no other place could ever do, from the sacred to the profane.

Even though my mother died a few short months ago, I feel so rich and overflowing with life. Her death has given me something I never thought possible. Deep in the unfathomable well of grief, I saw a glimmer of light, of hope, of my own resurrection.

My mother's death has invoked a new birth, a rebirth, day after day, moment by moment, an experience of life and self always new. This *rinascita*, my own personal Renaissance, is the soul of my travels, taking me deeper with every step, open and available to the world around me and within me.

Although I may resort to some old but comforting habits now and then, even those that don't truly serve me, I am always at choice. Each day I can connect with the greater power that turns the heavens, that orchestrates our lives. Each day I can shine my light a little brighter, illuminating the way into new and unknown adventures, this continual discovery of life, love and *la bella Italia.*

~ To be continued ~

Acknowledgments

It is with great honor that I mention the people who were actively part of my travels, who supported me, hosted me, became my friends, and showed a tremendous hospitality and generosity of spirit.

ENGLAND: My hosts Julie Fox, Anne Kearsley and Terhi Makela in and around Oxford for being so kind and helpful when I felt lost. • John & Elaine von Nuding for accepting my housesitting request in Suffolk and being so generous and flexible. • My nieces Mona and Zoe for providing the urn for my mother's ashes. • My brothers Richard and Jonathan for sharing the family journey with me.

DENMARK: My hosts Troels & Sherry List, Knud Riishojgaard & Malene Bichel and Jannick & Lotte Rosenlund for their warmth, humor and generosity and for becoming my friends. It is with a sad and heavy heart that I write Knud passed away during the editing of this book. He is greatly missed. • Allan Harsbro for his advice and help in tracking down my ancestor's birthplace, my Danish genealogy back to the 15th century and for introducing me to life on Aero. • Anette Hallstrom for her housesit and hospitality in the leafy suburbs north of Copenhagen. • My Danish relatives Natalie & Bjarne, Anna Cathrine & Kai, Erik & Inger, Christian & Tina, Jesper & Kis, Dayu, Suzanne, Michael and Axel (RIP).

ITALY: Silvia Bagnoli for her generosity and lifelong friendship, for sharing meals and letting me stay in her family villa in Tuscany. • Sophie Chamberlain for hosting me in her Tuscan villa apartment and for being a lifelong friend, along with her giant dog, Paco, may he rest in peace. • Gianni Sangalli for his humor and showing me the secrets of San Gimignano and Paola Morrazoni for her delicious coffee. • Marco Milli for his couch in Florence, his kindness, his cooking and the death-defying ride up to Fiesole. • Judith Munat for being an engaging and well-informed host, inviting me to a Florentine garden party and introducing me to the multi-layered history of Palermo. • Angela for renting me her bedroom in Florence, for conversations over dinner and for helping me speak Italian. • Alessia la Cava for hosting me in Rome, for her generosity and refreshing spirit, for long talks about life, for her recouped kitchen and throwing me a birthday dinner party on her roof. • Giangi Giardino for educating me about Naples and its history and for joining me on the Ciemmona. • Victoria King for hosting me in Rome, for sunsets on her beautiful terrace and for educating me about the realities of life in Italy. • Manuela and the staff of I Fiori di Napoli B&B for making me feel at home in the heart of Naples and advice on getting around the city and the Campania coast. • Alessandro at Bassani Space hair salon, Naples, for making me look and feel like an Italian. • Valeria Tondi for her authentic Neapolitan company over dinner on her balcony. • Caterina for renting me her beautiful flat in Palermo, for introducing me to her seafaring friends and being so kind to me when I needed it.

Simon Sebag Montefiore for his compelling BBC series, Rome: The Eternal City. It reawakened my deep-rooted connection to the city and the memories of being there just over three months before. This was the first sign I knew I was to return.

Andrew Graham-Dixon and Giorgio Locatelli for their BBC series, Italy Unpacked, a cultural road trip sharing the art, history and food of the regions, cities and towns they stopped in. Their exuberant celebration of Italy over four series greatly influenced my travels and appreciation of the country and its people.

Peter Robb for his detailed and deeply insightful account

of life in Palermo and Naples and the history of the mafia in his book, Midnight in Sicily.

Couchsurfing.com - This global hospitality network based on mutual trust, honesty, friendship and cultural exchange is the best form of travel I've experienced and enabled me to make friends around the world. Don't be fooled by the title—I only slept on one couch the entire time and even that was comfortable. The hosts I chose had spare rooms and even second homes. I felt treated like a king.

TrustedHousesitters.com - The most reliable and professional online service providing short to long-term housesitting for the global traveler. Thanks to them, I've had the good fortune to meet some wonderful people, look after some incredible properties and take care of some sweet animals during my assignments. I get to live like a local and integrate into communities wherever I go.

Heartfelt thanks to Glenn Berkenkamp for his insightful story editing, continued support and friendship; and Punya Kaufeler for her expert copy editing, multi-lingual proofreading skills and her friendship.

Special thanks goes to Julie Fox in Oxford, England, for providing the space and support I needed to finish this book.

About the Author

Born in England of British, Scottish and Danish descent, Navyo Ericsen has travel and adventure in his blood.

His Danish ancestor, Hans Halmøe Erichsen, was a member of the 1879 USS *Jeannette* Polar Expedition, the first official U.S. mission to the arctic. Only a handful survived. In 1890, each of the crew was awarded a congressional medal for bravery. The silver medal posthumously awarded to Hans has been handed down to Navyo and is a constant reminder of his heritage.

But it wasn't always that way.

With a training in classical music, his life has been filled with creativity that includes classical violist, rock musician, audio engineer, record producer, independent filmmaker and graphic designer. It is only later in life he has found writing and photography a means of expression and, most importantly, a means of sharing his adventures.

At the age of twenty-two, he traveled to India which changed the course of his life. Learning various methods of meditation, he spent decades exploring the inner world, giving him a keen insight into the human condition.

Based in Marin County, California since 1998, he now spends much of his time in Europe which provides the settings for his travelogues and photographs.

Navyo uses travel as a means of connection, education and discovery, immersing himself in the local language, customs and culture and integrating into community life. His travels have taken him from Scotland to Sicily, from Copenhagen to Crete and the many places in between.

But it is Italy with its diverse regions and landscape, rich history and culture, laid-back lifestyle, mouthwatering food and most of all its people that has captured his heart.

Also by Navyo Ericsen:
Soul Traveler Vol. 1: Taking the Jump

NavyoEricsen.com
Facebook.com/NavyoEricsenWriter
500px.com/NavyoEricsen/galleries

Printed in Great Britain
by Amazon

61167213R00166